JUSTICE *for* Blake

The Case of Home Sweet Home

A D. J. Douglas Investigative Adventure

A New Adventure Series

D.A. Bollen

PAGE PUBLISHING
Conneaut Lake, PA

First originally published by Page Publishing 2022

ISBN 979-8-88654-185-4 (pbk)
ISBN 979-8-88654-195-3 (digital)

Printed in the United States of America

CHAPTER 1

A Great Way to Start the Day!

I pressed the button on the box. A voice came back, "Identify yourself and purpose."

I answered, "D. J. Douglas, D. J.'s Bail Bonds. Here to surrender my bond on an inmate."

The security gate clicked open, and I entered the double-fenced-in area. The area to the left is for male inmates; to the right is for females…I head to the right.

One of my female *skips* was arrested the night before on her normal drug charges. When she *jumped bail*…skipped…, my $10,000 bond was forfeited by the court…and a warrant was issued for her arrest.

Now that she's back in custody, I'm sure the jail will find her warrant, but…I need to make sure my forfeited $10,000 bond gets addressed by the judge when she returns to court tomorrow.

So…here I am…to surrender the bail bond. The security door to this section of the detention facility buzzes…I push the door open, enter, place my keys in a basket, and pass through their security checkpoint. Clear!

I greet all of the deputies good morning and proceed to walk to the counter where I submit my bond surrender paperwork.

To my right are four *holding cells* that contain females recently arrested, waiting to be processed and assigned to more permanent accommodations!

I see my deputy buddy behind the counter and wave my paperwork. He nods his head…but tilts it to the right…teasing me to look!

Following his direction, I take a quick glance…OMG! The third *holding cell* is an *ocean of white*! The white fabric, a wedding gown, was pressing against the bars in the cell looking for an avenue of escape!

I laughed to myself, smiled at my buddy, and handed him my paperwork when I reached his counter.

We both, being professional, had to laugh quietly. We have seen these situations before: *jailhouse weddings!* But…this one didn't happen. Evidently the bride-to-be had three warrants on her. When she showed her ID to the deputy to gain access to the detention facility, they input her name into the computer to verify her ID…and who would have thought, the warrants popped up! She was arrested immediately and placed in the holding cell for further processing! Remarkable! Amazing!

After handing the paperwork to my friend, I asked him for the name of this *lady*. I certainly didn't want to post any bond on her!

Having had a good chuckle to get my morning started, I thanked my friend as he gave me back a certified copy of my paperwork, which I needed for my records. I waved goodbye and retraced my steps to exit the facility.

This detention facility, the local jail, is only three blocks from my office…a short ten-minute walk. While making this quick trek back to the office, I'm calculating that my *lady fugitive/skip* will be taken to court tomorrow morning, and my $10,000 forfeited liability will be cleared at that time.

It was a good morning's work…plus, *I got some free entertainment!* And…I like *anything* free!

* * *

It's 7:45 a.m. Marla, my accounts receivable manager and night owl, who handles the office during the night, left a little earlier. Nelly, my office manager, showed up for her shift before Marla left. She updated her on the night's activities…who's scheduled to come in to complete their paperwork, any new bonds needing to be posted… the usual!

Between the three of us, we make sure this office runs like a Swiss clock! We've been together since I opened the office twenty years ago! We have perfected our systems over the years: posting bonds, collecting on accounts, and most importantly, apprehending those who *jump bail!*

While we handle the office, my team of five investigators…a.k.a. bounty hunters…concentrate on our fugitive cases. The investigators have been with me for over eight years…and have a very impressive arrest record!

I have *really* been in the bail industry for over thirty years! My uncle Mike brought me into his business when I was sixteen years old…teaching me everything! I worked for him on the weekends when I was in high school and then full-time after I graduated from college, with an emphasis on business / criminal justice. He would always tell me to take care of my clients, my staff, and our community! Those were the three ingredients necessary to guarantee a successful business…and life!

Uncle Mike retired from our local sheriff's department over thirty-five years ago. I remember the days when he would take me to the karate studio to train with him…and to the shooting range! If I was going to run my own bail agency, he wanted to make sure I was able to handle myself in any given situation. He always loved the bail business but also knew the risks taken every day…and had to be prepared to cope with any situation which may arise! Thanks, Uncle Mike!

* * *

Nelly is busy at her desk reviewing the notes Marla left her… getting ready for the day! I take a seat at her desk and hand her the paperwork from the jail, certifying our bond surrender. She will contact the court tomorrow afternoon to make sure our forfeited bond was cleared. Smiling, I told her about the *jailhouse wedding* escapade…and the free entertainment that started my day! Now I need to get down to business.

I called Donny, my lead investigator, and told him I had completed the bond surrender so he could close out this case. Donny and his team handle an average of twenty investigative cases at any given point in time. Each member of the team, with their law enforcement background, possesses their own individual talent and style. When they get together on a case, their combined specialties make them unstoppable!

Before I head to my desk, I stop and get my morning cup of coffee. Getting comfortable, I look out over my office with pride! It appears to be inviting to our potential clients, and very professional. I glance at our *photo wall*, which displays the pictures of Marla, Nelly, myself, and a variety of scenery shots. These scenery pictures depict the locations of some of our adventures: the Chapel of Perpetual Love in Las Vegas and a French Villa in Paris. Not that I label these pictures, they simply add color to the wall. Besides, my staff and investigators know the locations and the adventures we had at each! Just a friendly reminder for all of us…which always brings a smile to our faces!

Nelly breaks my reverie by telling me she is expecting some potential clients in soon. Two separate families…one family wishing to bail out their daughter on drug charges, a $15,000 bail; and the other family just wanting information, not quite sure they want to bail their son out, again…a $25,000 for burglary. I told Nelly she can handle the first family, and I would talk to the second.

When someone makes an appointment with us to discuss bail for their loved one, we always contact the jail and get the inmate's information…DOB, charges, bail amount, and whether the case is a felony or misdemeanor. Having this information ahead of the meeting saves us time, and we can focus on the family…are they able to pay the premium for the bail, do they live local, and would they make sure their loved one attends all the court hearings? Just the basic info for now!

When someone contacts our office for bail, we don't care if they are guilty or innocent. That's up to the court. We do care about the defendant/client making all their court appearances…and will we have to go looking for them! Which costs me money! Essentially, will they be responsible for their bail…and me?

While waiting for the families to show up, I called Donny and asked him if he could come to the office at about two o'clock to discuss the cases currently under investigation. No problem…he'll get updates from everyone on their cases and see me at two o'clock.

As expected, both of the families showed up twenty minutes later. Nelly and I introduced ourselves and welcomed them. One family went with Nelly, and I directed the other family to my desk.

We took our time with each family, fully explaining the bail process: what was their responsibility, the client's responsibility, and the bail premium. They each decided to proceed with posting the bail for their family members. Now the paperwork end of the process starts…which only takes twenty minutes. Nelly's family produces cash for the 10 percent premium, $1,500. My family writes me a check for $2,500…and we, naturally, call the bank to confirm the funds are available. All is good.

We told our new clients that the bonds will be posted within thirty minutes, and their family members released within two to three hours. I reminded them I expected their loved ones to be in my office no later than two hours after their release…they had to complete their part of the bail application. Both families promised to have them here as soon as possible.

Nelly and I shook their hands and thanked them for their business: they were in good hands.

I called the jail to confirm the information that was necessary for each bail bond: inmate's name, charges, bail amount, and court appearance date. Nelly was preparing the bond paperwork, with all the relevant information. Once completed, I smiled at Nelly…and flipped a coin to see which one of us would run the paperwork to the jail. She called heads…it came up tails…so I won the toss…and get the break!

It's only 12:30 p.m…so I have plenty of time to get the bonds posted before my meeting with Donny. Nelly hands me the paper-work, and I head to the jail, three blocks away.

With the bonds now posted, I figured my *new clients* should be at the office no later than 6:30 p.m. to complete their portion of the paperwork. We'll keep an eye open for them.

I get back to the office…it's 1:15 p.m. Donny will be here in forty-five minutes to go over all the cases…so I head to the confer-ence room and get it set up for us…need lots of room to spread out. Nelly put on a fresh pot of coffee! So thoughtful!

While I'm preparing the conference room, Nelly is entering all the information on our two new bonds into the computer.

Aside from the music coming from Marla's boom box, it is pretty quiet in the office…we're both doing busy work…in case any poten-tial client walks into the office…always have to look professional!

CHAPTER 2

Keeping Ahead of the Game!

Both Donny and his partner, Steve, arrive at the office a little early...1:50 p.m. They stopped off and picked up sandwiches for everyone...they were hungry and figured we would be too! So sweet! They both give Nelly a hug, leave a sandwich on her desk, and then head back to the conference room.

Steve grabs some plates and napkins from the kitchen and sets everything on the conference table. We get situated around the table and grab a sandwich. I have my notepad ready...Donny and Steve pull the files from their briefcases. We're now ready for anything!

Donny starts the meeting. We currently have twenty cases under investigation, which total $530,000 in forfeited liability. Ten of the cases are with him and Steve, Darren, and Gina are working their magic on the ten remaining cases. Donny acknowledged the earlier bond surrender at the jail...so he and Steve now have nine cases... which brings our liability to $520,000.

Steve jumps in to continue the report. He was confident six of the nine cases will be closed over the next two to three weeks. They are developing some great *intel* on them, bringing them closer each day. Their remaining three cases will take a little more investigation...he expects they will have them closed over the next two months. He added these fugitives are changing locations practically every day...to stay ahead of us and law enforcement...and friends are hiding them. But we've dealt with these circumstances before…and we always win! I like their positive attitude!

Donny takes over again. Now on to Darren and Gina. Darren, being the *skip-tracing* expert, and Gina, being a *chameleon*, are gathering some terrific information on their cases. They estimated nine of their cases will be cleared within the next two months, some maybe in the next couple of weeks. However, Donny is really smiling now; he tells me they are currently sitting on a location for one of their female fugitives…and they *know* she is there…they saw her go into her mother's house, and she has not come out! They are watching patiently!

Donny, still smiling, asks me if I want to be in on the action. This is a $100,000 forfeited liability…you bet I would love to be *in on the action*! Steve gathers up the files and a sandwich for the road. I grab my ID and tell Nelly what's going on…we'll be back as soon as possible.

The three of us climb into Donny's car, head to the location, and meet up with Darren and Gina. Gina gives us a rundown of our lady fugitive: Christine Campbell, thirty-seven years old, five feet four, 130 pounds, short brown hair. They saw her enter her mother's property two hours earlier…and has not left. The car she came in is parked in front of the house. The mother, Caroline Campbell, is sixty years of age.

I commented this area appears to be quite affluent…well-kept homes, yards, etc. Very expensive homes in this community. Darren agreed, stating our *skip* had been the office manager for a local real estate company and was charged with grand theft. She had stolen, over a period of six months, $100,000, from the real estate agency… plus the theft of a variety of documents and company property!

Normally, when a person *jumps bail*, the judge issues a warrant and doubles the original bail amount for the warrant. So…our lady has a $200,000 warrant on her head! And our forfeiture notice, issued by the court, is our warrant, allowing us great latitude for the fugitive's apprehension.

Shortly after Darren and Gina arrived at this location, hours earlier, she contacted the local law enforcement agency to check in with them. She gave the fugitive's name and location. The desk sergeant acknowledged the warrant and advised her to call should they need additional backup.

Now we're ready…how do we want to proceed? We decided to wait another thirty minutes…to see if she would emerge from the house. If she didn't, then we would door knock! Simple!

No movement…no sign of her…car is still parked in front of the house. The five of us climbed out of Donny's car and approached the house…with our warrant and IDs in hand.

Donny knocks on the door. No answer…but we hear movement inside. He knocks again…still no answer. He knocks again… and identifies himself. The mother finally answers the door…Donny asks for her daughter. She states that she has not seen her daughter for over a month! Donny shows her our warrant and asks her to step aside…we will be searching her home. He also mentions something about *aiding and abetting* to the mother! This didn't faze her one bit!

We split up to search the house…Donny and Steve took the upstairs and Darren, Gina, and I the downstairs. We checked out all the rooms…even the attic…and there was no sign of this lady! *How could that be…we knew she was here!*

Once our respective searches were done, we met up in the kitchen to compare notes. The mother was standing outside the home while we conducted our search. Donny and Steve didn't see any belongings in the spare bedroom that might belong to our fugitive. No purse, cell phone, or keys. Darren, Gina, and I reported the same…nothing…no sign of her. But…we knew she was here…*but where?*

The one area we had not checked yet was the garage…located off the kitchen. Darren opened the door that led from the kitchen to the garage. We entered the garage, noting how clean it looked… everything in place, the lawn mower to the right, hedge clippers hanging on the wall, and a mixture of other yard implements hanging from hooks on the wall…but no sign of our lady! Parked in the garage was a relatively new Mercedes-Benz…one with all the bells and whistles. Beautiful! Gina found the button for the electric garage door and pushed it. The door came up smoothly, showing the driveway which led to the street where the lady's car was parked. We never saw her come out of the garage, and her car was still there. We were all scratching our heads…what was going on…what are we missing?

We're all standing at the opening of the garage, behind the parked Mercedes, discussing our options. Steve, all of a sudden, holds up his hand and places his finger on his lips…signaling us to be quiet! Then we heard it…a ringing! The ringing of a cell phone… and it was coming from the trunk of the Mercedes! Gina walked quietly to the front of the Mercedes, opened the driver's door, and found the trunk release latch. She looked at us…we were in position, surrounding the back end of the car. She pulled the latch and up pops the trunk lid! Inside was our lady, coiled up in a fetal position, holding her cell phone! Donny identified himself, and the team helped her out of the car, placed the handcuffs on her, and put her in the back seat of his car. While walking her to his car, he told her that he hoped that phone call was an important one…because she won't be getting any more calls for quite some time!

Meanwhile, the mother is in the front yard, trying to make a spectacle of herself. Gina approached her and told her to settle down…that if she wanted Gina would place a call to the police and ask them to arrest her for *aiding and abetting* her daughter…which carried a jail term of five years…is that what she wanted? The mother immediately shut up!

Donny and Steve drive off with our fugitive to book her into our local jail. Darren, Gina, and I head back to the office. Another case closed out…and a big one at that! I told them thanks for letting me come along for the ride…it was so much fun. I can't do it all the time, but I love getting some action now and then!

Gina and Darren drop me off at the office. Nelly is waiting anxiously to hear how things went. I told her *case closed*! I gave her a brief rundown of how we couldn't find her anywhere in the house… searched it from top to bottom! But, nothing! She was looking at me with curious eyes. I told her once we got into the garage, everything looked in its proper place…even the Mercedes-Benz was parked perfectly! It was when Steve heard a ringing sound…coming from the trunk of the Mercedes. We popped the trunk and guess who we found! Nelly was shaking her head…amazed at the lengths people will go to…with the help of mothers!

I told her Donny was booking her into the jail now, and she will be going to court tomorrow. I asked Nelly to check the court tomorrow afternoon to make sure our $100,000 forfeited liability got cleared. It would be her pleasure. Another case to close out! Only eighteen cases left…for the time being.

CHAPTER 3

Business As Usual?

It's been a pretty busy day…and really productive…we closed out two cases…$110,000 of liability! While Nelly is updating the computer, she starts laughing and asks me if I got a picture of the Mercedes-Benz…to add to our photo wall! I don't think so! If it had been a Rolls-Royce Sweptail I might have considered!

With nothing exciting going on at the moment, we fell into our routine. Nelly is checking on the bond status of several of our clients…to see if their cases are completed…and our bonds exonerated/cleared. If our clients make all of their scheduled court appearances and are sentenced on their case, the case is closed. The courts will have all the relevant information.

While Nelly is working with the courts, I decided to run our daily report which lists our outstanding liability, shows upcoming court dates for our clients, and provides me with an update of our accounts receivable. Everything is looking really good. Ninety-nine percent of our clients are making their court appearances…and are paying their bills!

It's the remaining 1 percent of our clients that we spend 50 percent of our time on: our fugitives! But…that's half the fun…outsmarting the criminals…and I have the perfect team!

My thought process comes to an end as Marla walks through the door. She immediately walks to her boom box and changes the station to her rock and roll. Nelly is trying to hide at her desk…she forgot to put on a fresh pot of coffee for Marla…oops! We don't ask for much out of life…except our music and coffee!

Marla is muttering to herself…and giggling at the same time! She's trying to be a martyr…but it's not working! Nelly finished up her court calls…and we have twelve cases/bonds out of fifteen closed out. That's great news. She'll run over to the court tomorrow and get the proof we need for our records.

After Marla put on her pot of coffee, she sat with Nelly to find out what happened during the day and what to expect for the evening. My gals! I hear the Swiss clock ticking as it should!

As I'm getting ready to call it a day myself, Donny calls me on my cell phone. He wanted me to know our $100,000 skip, Christine Campbell, is booked into jail and scheduled to appear in court tomorrow. He has his copy of the booking sheet and will drop it off at the office in the morning. Thanks, Donny…well done.

Before Nelly and I could leave the office, Marla runs over and gives us each a big hug. I know the office is in good hands for the evening…she has her boom box and coffee…she's livin' the dream! Everything is as it should be!

* * *

I get into the office at 6:30 a.m. Marla looks fresh as a peach! Her rock and roll music playing in the background and half a pot of coffee is on the burner. She had a great night: our new clients from yesterday came in and completed their part of the paperwork, she lined up three families to come in this morning to discuss bailing out their friends, and she was able to enter client info into the computer. *She did have a great night!*

After dropping her kids off at school, Nelly arrived at 7:30 a.m…carrying a box of donuts…the main food group for bail agents! We gathered around Nelly's desk with our donut and coffee…and jibber-jabbering about the *lady in the trunk* adventure from yesterday…laughing about the extremes people will go to avoid arrest!

With that, Marla bid us farewell. Nelly and I were ready for anything the day would bring! Or so I thought…

I make my way back to my desk and get comfortable in my ratty chair. I look at the pile of mail sitting in my inbox…two days' worth of mail. As always, the usual: bills, junk mail, and some very nice thank-you cards! I didn't see any notices from the court…which made me happy. No clients have missed court yet! But I know things will change…they always do!

As I finished up the mail, Donny walks in and hands Nelly the booking sheet on the *trunk fugitive*, Christine Campbell. He spots the donuts, grabs one, and comes back to my desk. In between bites, he asks me if I would like a German shepherd puppy…maybe a mascot for the office! He adds that he has a job for me and Gina…a fun job and one that wouldn't put me in harm's way…I would be quite safe. Always curious about these requests from him…I asked him to tell me more about this upcoming adventure.

As we know, Darren and Steve are the experts on social media. Whenever we get a new case for investigation, they immediately delve into the world of ether…checking on the various media platforms. It's amazing what people put on the Internet: who they're dating, what restaurants they like, when they go to the beach, where they're vacationing, when they're getting married and where doggies are for sale!

Apparently, Steve found one of his *bail jumpers* had posted an ad on one of the media platforms: German shepherd puppies for sale, eight weeks old. Please call 562-555-1737 to set an appointment.

This particular *skip* is a $15,000 liability, with a $30,000 warrant. Steve wants Gina and me to set an appointment with him to see his puppies. He feels women are less intimidating, and our fugitive would not be expecting to get arrested! So true!

I'm in…let's call Gina and see when would be a good time for her! Donny gets her on the phone, Gina's in…and we decided on 6:00 p.m…we'll tell him we can swing by his place after work. Done.

So…I call our *skip*. It's nine thirty in the morning; let's see if he answers…maybe he's at work…yeah, right! He picks up the phone on the third ring. I tell him I saw his ad about puppies for sale and was wondering if I could come by after work, probably around six, to see the precious puppies…I also asked how much he was selling the puppies for. He said six o'clock would be a great time…and he was asking $250 for the puppy because they are purebred! I pretended to get all excited. I asked him to give me his address…which he did! I continued my babble saying I'm looking forward to seeing him later…and I'll bring cash! Our *date* is now set…time and location!

Donny called Gina and confirmed our *date*. We decided Gina and I would arrive at his location first, with Donny and Steve following us. Gina and I would be the *bait*, and once he came out to show us his puppies, Donny and Steve would snag him. Sounds like a good plan to me. Gina said she would pick me up at the office at five, and we would head out then. Donny checked the address our *skip* gave us…it was totally different from what we had on his application! Good thing he has puppies for sale! This makes it so much easier!

I now have some *fun* to look forward to! But that's seven hours away. Everything is running smoothly this morning. One of the families Marla set up to come in and discuss bailing out their daughter arrived an hour ago…and sat with Nelly. Being ever so professional, Nelly was ready for them: had the jail printout detailing the charges and bail amount. It was a $20,000 bail and drug charges. She went over the bail process with them…explaining their responsibilities, their daughter's responsibilities to them, and to us. The family seemed confident she would abide by all the conditions. Great. Nelly completed the paperwork and received their check for the 10 percent premium.

While Nelly was finishing up with our new clients, I put on a fresh pot of coffee…no donuts were left…rats! I look around the office and see a couple of files on Marla's desk that need to be placed in the file cabinets. And per our usual protocol, while the family is still here, Nelly called the bank to confirm the funds were available… they were…perfect!

I walked up to Marla's desk to grab the files and introduced myself to our new clients. Shaking their hands, I told them we appreciated their business and, should they have any questions, to just give us a call…we are here for them!

The coffee is done…Nelly has finished filling out the bail bond…ready to be posted with the jail! I get myself a cup of coffee and head back to place the files in the cabinets, dropping off my coffee at my desk. Knowing she probably would love a break…it's always nice to get out of the office for a while…I ask Nelly if she would like to run the bail bond over to the jail. I can handle the office. She accepts my offer…reminding me that we have two more families set to come in. I got it! And, oh, one more thing: could you swing by the bank and deposit the check to make sure they don't place a *stop payment* on it…you bet! Gotta protect ourselves!

* * *

Over the next three hours, the two other families made it in…both decided to proceed with the bail. I worked with one of the families and Nelly with the other…what a team! A total of $65,000 in bail…we'll take it! So far, it's been a great morning: $85,000 in bail for the day. All the paperwork was completed, the premium monies received, and the bonds posted with the jail.

It's four…only have an hour to wait for our next fun *adventure*! Relaxing a bit, Nelly and I talk about our upcoming *doggie* ruse…adding we don't need an office mascot! As we're kicking back, John, our mailman, comes in and hands me a stack of mail. It looks like the usual stuff…mainly junk mail. I do see an envelope, the type I don't particularly like seeing: a letter from the court! Nuts…that means we have a forfeited bail bond…a *skip*. Ripping off the end of the envelope, I pull the notice out and review it completely. First off, I see I have a $150,000 bond which was forfeited four days prior. The name is Blake Beaumont. I have Nelly pull up the client's account on our computer and see that Ms. Beaumont has been making her court appearances for the last four months. Something must have happened…she was probably getting close to being sentenced…and didn't want to go to jail!

We review her charges and personal information to get a better understanding of our new *skip*. The charges were for *title theft*. She liked to steal the homes/property of other people! She lived locally

and at one point was employed in the real estate industry. Hmmm…
something familiar with this scenario!

Gina, Donny, and Steve get to the office. Nelly and I are still
reviewing her information. I tell the team we have a new $150,000
skip…but we'll go over it later. Nelly starts printing out everything
from the computer and calls the jail to make arrangements to pick up
copies of her booking photo and warrant.

While the team and I are getting ready to head out, Marla arrives
and sees the commotion in the office. Nelly brings her up-to-date on
our new *skip* and the puppy *ruse* we are getting ready to initiate. I
ask my gals to get with Darren to run a comprehensive background
check on Blake Beaumont: employment records, banking, travels,
and all known residences. And whatever else they can come up with.

Now it's time to concentrate on our $15,000 *skip*. We've
reviewed the action plan, and Donny provided us with his stats: thir-
ty-three-year-old male, five feet eight, 160 pounds, shaggy brown
hair, no facial hair. Steve ran a quick Internet search on the address
he gave us, and it appears to be the home of his father. We'll have to
be alert to that fact!

We pile into our respective cars and head out…Gina and I are
in the lead with the guys following. It's five fifty…we arrived a little
early. We find a place to park across from the target residence and the
guys pull in four car lengths behind us.

Gina and I jump out of the car…acting very excited…in case
he happens to be watching us from inside the house. As we are walking up to the front door, the garage door opens…and we can hear
the puppies crying and barking. A *gentleman* steps over to the walk-
way and introduces himself…yep! Our fugitive! He welcomes us and
directs us to his garage where we see six puppies playing and trying to
get out of a large cardboard box. We approach the puppy box, with
our arms extended…reach in and pick up one of the pups. *They are
so cute!* Gina is engaging him in a conversation about the puppies:
how old, do they have their shots, are you sure they are purebred? As
we are talking with him, we are slowly leading him outside the garage
to the driveway…where I see Donny and Steve walking leisurely in
front of the house…just out for a stroll!

I walk back to the puppy box and put my pup back in. As I'm returning to the garage, I try to see if there is any activity coming from the house…maybe his dad is watching the transaction…but I don't see any movement. Gina is still in the driveway talking business. She reaches into her pocket, hoping the man will think she is reaching for her money. Knowing she has this man baited, she nods her head…and Donny and Steve quietly approach. With handcuffs at the ready, Donny identifies himself and the team and places him under arrest. Our *skip* was surprised we found him…he thought by changing his locations frequently, he was safe! He, naturally, blamed it on the puppies! If he hadn't told his dad he would sell them for him, he'd still be free! As Donny is placing him in the back of his car, he looks back at Gina and me and asks, "Do you still want to buy a puppy?"

Well, the guys are on their way to book our *skip* into jail. Gina and I get back to the office. Gina gives Nelly and Marla a quick rundown of the events…nothing too exciting! Just your normal, non-eventful, takedown! But…it's another case closed.

My gals told me they contacted Darren for the detailed *skip-tracing* request…never a problem. He should have some results for us in the morning. Nelly handed me copies of everything we had on the computer on her. Marla said she made arrangements for us to pick up the copies of her booking photo and warrant tomorrow morning. Job well done! Another fun and exciting day. And…more to come.

Gina, Nelly, and I have been going for fourteen hours…time for us to get home! I told them we'll get together tomorrow afternoon to review the information on our new $150,000 *skip*. I'll try to get everyone in…and, yes, there will be food!

CHAPTER 4

The Gang of Eight!

I get into the office at 6:30 a.m., my usual time. I didn't get much sleep…I couldn't turn my brain off! Lots of questions that I need answers to…and will get!

Marla was working on inputting information into the computer. She had made copies of the Blake Beaumont application and any additional information we had in her file.

After giving her my morning hug, I asked her if she could print out all of the information we had on Christine Campbell…and make copies of that also. She looked at me kind of funny, knowing that we had recently arrested Ms. Campbell and our bond…our $100,000 forfeited liability…had been cleared a couple of days ago. I told her I would explain later…it was a feeling I had to follow up on!

I poured myself a cup of her famous coffee and headed to my desk. I needed to make some notes…the thoughts that kept rattling around in my brain all night!

- Get with Bill Baxter, district attorney
- Need complete court files on Christine Campbell and Blake Beaumont, including all court dockets
- Need a list of *known associates* on both Campbell and Beaumont…DA Baxter may be able to help with that info

- Are any of the known associates in custody? What is their current status?

I know there's more, but this is a good start. I called Donny and asked him if he and the team could be at the office at 1:00 p.m. for a meeting. I told him Darren is running an in-depth background check on Ms. Beaumont, and he should have the info by then so we can all review it. I also asked Donny if he could ask him to run an additional background check on Christine Campbell…and have that info for the meeting as well. He said he'd let everyone know… and, yes, sandwiches would be just fine! He mentioned he has the booking sheet for our *doggie* guy and will give it to Nelly when he gets in. Great!

Marla finished making the copies on Campbell just as Nelly walked through the door. Knowing that Marla is off-shift shortly, I told them I scheduled a meeting with everyone for one o'clock to discuss this Beaumont case. I asked Marla, with a loving smile, if she would be up to joining us…and, yes, food will be provided. That's all it took…she'll be here…she didn't want to miss out on anything!

She took all of her copies to the conference room and spread them out on the table. I planned on reviewing them shortly after I made some phone calls.

It wasn't quite 8:00 a.m. The court opens at eight. I asked Nelly to run over to the court and get complete copies of the case files on Campbell and Beaumont. Copies of everything in their file… no matter how trivial! She snagged a cup of coffee for the road and headed over to the courthouse.

I needed to make two phone calls: (1) Bill Baxter, my DA friend, and (2) David Williams, my part-time Investigator in Northern California.

I called DA Baxter first, just in case he needed to run to court. I was greeted with his normal warm welcome. I told him I needed a big favor: could he possibly provide me with a list of *known associates* for Christine Campbell and Blake Beaumont? I reminded him we had recently arrested Ms. Campbell and were now looking for Ms. Beaumont. I explained that I had one of my strange feelings about these women and just needed to confirm some thoughts…and, besides, we're doing the work on bringing these rascals to justice! He laughed and said he can have his secretary pull the information in an hour or so…and I can pick it up at about 11:00 a.m. Perfect! We work so well together…I help him…he helps me!

Next, I needed to reach out to David Williams…*Professor David Williams…Sergeant David Williams*! David came to us six months ago. He and Donny were old friends, having been on the same police force twelve years ago. When Donny was with the police force in Northern California, he also taught criminal justice classes at the local university, Collier University. He came to work for me eight years ago, and David took over teaching his criminal justice classes. Although he is a tenured professor at the university, he maintained his standing with the local police agency, joining the *reserve* division.

Seven months ago, the team and I had a $500,000 *skip* which led us from Southern California to Paris to Northern California. David was very instrumental in helping us close the case! Plus, he had a lot of fun. I asked him then if he would be interested in helping us out from time to time on our cases…thankfully, he said he would be honored! Over the last three to four months, he's assisted us on some minor cases…which was great! Now…we have another case which will require his assistance and brilliance!

Looking forward to talking to him, I placed the call to his cell phone. It's 9:00 a.m…he may not be in class yet! David answered almost immediately, not a "Hi. How are you?"…just an "It's about time you called me!" I was trying to stop laughing! But that's what made David so endearing…he always cut to the chase.

I asked him how his schedule looked for the near future… explaining our $150,000 case…what we knew so far. I told him the team and I were having a brainstorming meeting at one in an attempt to generate some solid information…give us some direction! I didn't need him right now, but probably in the next couple of days. He mentioned the university was on break for the next couple of weeks, and he just has to stay in touch with the police department in case anything arises. I was very happy! I told him I would have Donny call him tonight, and we can make plans on him joining us for some more fun! Agreed! He can't wait to hear from Donny!

Nelly returned from the courthouse…it took forever to find the files, let alone have copies made. She was carrying a stack of papers no less than eight inches thick! This is going to be interesting! I asked her if she could make copies for everyone…no problem. Good thing we have lots of copy paper!

While she's making the copies, I tell her about my conversations with DA Baxter and David…and about some of my thoughts! She gets a silly grin on her face…saying that Gina will be happy to *work* with David again! We both laugh a little…knowing that a budding romance is developing! Good for them!

However, she was wondering *why* the court files on Campbell and Beaumont…now it made perfect sense…and…how did I ever think of it! I told her something was bothering me…the little hairs on the back of my neck were standing up…I knew we needed to run my thoughts to the ground to see if I am right! No time to waste!

* * *

I glanced at the clock on the wall…OMG…ten fifty! I need to get over to the DA's office. Nelly, still making all the copies, can handle the office for a few minutes.

I walk into the office and see Susie, the DA's secretary, waving some papers at me. Susie has been with DA Baxter for over ten years! She is his go-to woman! After I give her a big hug, haven't seen her for a while, she hands me the papers…saying "How did I know?" I told her it was just a hunch that came to me in the middle of the night! She said I will find it very interesting! Holding back the urge to look at the papers, I thanked her and headed back to the office. We still had work to do before our one o'clock meeting!

OMG…I forgot…food! I quickly called the corner burger joint and placed my order…and we would pick it up at 12:45 p.m. No problem…it'll be ready and waiting!

I sat with Nelly at her desk…she was taking a well-deserved break from making *all* the copies! Lots and lots of copies…and paper!

Practically a whole ream of paper! Let alone making seven separate stacks…one copy for each of us.

Now looking over the papers that Susie had given me…I started nodding my head…I think I'm right! I gave the papers to Nelly to look at…and she was shocked at what she saw!

Being the considerate boss, I volunteered to make the copies for everyone. I wanted Nelly to rest! She's been going 200 percent since she walked in the door this morning!

Okay…so let's see what we have so far for everyone:

- Copies of our office files on Campbell and Beaumont
- Copies of the complete court files on both
- Copies of their *known associates* as provided by the DA
- Darren's background checks on both *ladies*

Whew! Now, I just wanted to check a couple more things with the jail. I can do that on the computer. I printed out the info I got from the jail website and, again, made copies for everyone…but I'm hanging on to this last nugget of information! Just for a while!

Darren and Gina arrived first. Darren had indeed done his homework! While he was making copies for everyone, I asked Gina if she could run and pick up our food order. No problem…she's out the door!

Nelly took all her copies and headed to the conference room. She saw the seven piles that Marla had started earlier. She placed her copies on each stack and tried to arrange them in the order we would be discussing them. Darren walked in with his copies and gave them to Nelly…they would be the second topic of discussion!

Let's see…who are we missing: Marla, Donny, and Steve…still a little early. I gathered some note pads and yellow highlighters from the storage cabinet and set one of each on top of the stack of papers. I know this meeting is going to get intense! However, productive!

The rest of the team show up just as Gina arrives with the food. I swear, they can smell a hamburger a mile away!

Everyone gets situated in the conference room…Nelly sets the buzzer on the front door…in case a client walks in while *we're hav-*

ing lunch! They see the stack of papers…and are looking at me with quizzical expressions on their faces…each a little daunted by the size of the stack!

Everyone has a hamburger and soda…so let's get started. First up…I tell them about our $150,000 forfeited liability…our new skip! Blake Beaumont. Marla directs their attention to the office file copy.

"Thirty-nine years of age, five feet seven, 140 pounds, short blonde hair…please see booking photo…and a rose tattoo on her right wrist. Not married. No children. Her charges are six counts of title fraud. She likes to steal the homes of hardworking people! She *was a real estate agent* for a variety of local real estate agencies over the last couple of years. The warrant for $300,000 has been issued. Please see a copy of the warrant in your file. The client paid the full premium, $15,000 by check, which cleared the bank. The cosignor on the bail bond is a Caroline Campbell."

Marla continues stating that she has not had time to conduct a preliminary investigation regarding friends, family, etc. But she will as the day progresses.

I can see my team making notes and highlighting items on the bail application…*especially the name of Christine Campbell*!

Next, we move on to the file for Christine Campbell: thirty-seven years old, five feet four, 130 pounds, short brown hair, no noticeable tattoos or scars. Divorced, no children. We arrested her two days ago at her mother's home, and our liability has been cleared with the court. She is currently in custody, with a $200,000 bail. Her charges were embezzlement from her employer plus the theft of company documents and company property. She, too, was employed by a local real estate office. The cosignor on her bond was a married couple: Rudolph and Judith Jameson. Their credit check came back *excellent*, and they, also, paid the premium in full with a check, which cleared the bank.

So far…so good! I can see their minds getting in sync with mine! I let them know we will not be going over every piece of paper in front of them…most of it is for their review and case file. We will just be touching on the most important items in each section.

Now, it's Darren's turn…he ran the comprehensive background check on both *ladies*. He brings their attention to his copies…pointing out a few items that he has already highlighted! Apparently, both *ladies* are members of the same gym…they have known each other for roughly four years. Ms. Campbell is listed as a Notary for the State of California; she worked at the same real estate agency for a little over four years, interacting with Ms. Beaumont from time to time!

Ms. Beaumont has a bachelor's degree in English from an East Coast University. She lived in Massachusetts for twelve years, prior to moving to our wonderful town; she has a checking and saving account with our local bank…however, the funds had been frozen pending the outcome of her court case. According to IRS records, she has worked for six different real estate companies over the last ten years.

Ms. Campbell only graduated high school and married a Spencer Campbell shortly after graduating. Their marriage only lasted two years. She was born and raised in our sweet little town; however, she does not have many friends. Because of their similar occupations, they became fast friends. Darren mentioned he had a chance to speak to her previous employer and asked if he had ever met a Blake Beaumont "Did she ever come to his office?" The employer relayed that he met her on a variety of occasions. "Company Christmas party, company outings, etc. And, yes, she probably had been to his office maybe five or six times over the years." Adding some not-so-nice comments about Ms. Campbell…something about rotting in jail!

So, as Darren continued, they did have a prior relationship… both somewhat personal and professional. Great job, Darren…we're getting our heads wrapped around these *ladies*.

Nelly takes the stage now! She pointed to the court case documents on each *lady*! The documents listed the *victims* of Beaumont's theft charges…the locations of the individual properties and the value of each property. Nelly asked us to review the court file later to get a feel for what was happening in each case. However, she wanted to point out the last couple of pages of Beaumont's court docket, which stated the district attorney was looking to send her to prison for a term of eight years and pay restitution to her many victims, in the amount of $2,888,000! She was to be sentenced on her next court appearance, which was when she failed to appear…and our bail bond was forfeited by the court! Wow! I see my team highlighting all this info!

I saved myself for last…because the information I have, that DA Baxter provided me, is a bombshell!

Before I started, I asked the team if they had any questions so far. They all shook their heads. Now, I passed out my copies…two pages in total. I explained that DA Baxter compiled this report for me. The report was simply entitled "Known Associates." The first page listed the known associates for *Christine Campbell*:

- Rudolph Jameson
- Judith Jameson
- Samuel Peyton
- Dean Caravello
- Sarah Vasquez
- Lisa Montgomery
- *Blake Beaumont*

The second page listed the known associates for *Blake Beaumont*:

- Rudolph Jameson
- Judith Jameson
- Samuel Peyton
- Dean Caravello
- Sarah Vasquez
- Lisa Montgomery
- *Christine Campbell*

The team was shocked! But I was not done yet! I did some research on the local jail website and found that Samuel Peyton, Dean Caravello, and Lisa Montgomery are currently in custody and have been ever since their arrest months ago. They were never bailed out!

I pointed out to the team that Christine Campbell's mother was the *cosignor* on Blake Beaumont's bond. And Rudolph and Judith Jameson (Rudy and Judy, how cute!) were the *cosignors* of Christine's bond. Are we seeing a pattern?

I asked everyone to go home and review this information…and maybe we can meet up tomorrow at about the same time to discuss a plan.

In addition to our fugitive Beaumont, we need to check on the whereabouts of Sarah Vasquez and the Jamesons.

And, oh, by the way, David has some time off from the university, so he'll be jumping in to help on this case. I asked Donny to give him a call tonight to bring him up to speed.

CHAPTER 5

Getting Our Ducks Lined Up!

It was a productive meeting…everyone remained in the conference room…discussing potential scenarios…what should be our next step? They studied the court dockets of both *ladies*, trying to get an idea of what was going on with their cases. They reviewed our bail applications that were filled out at the time we posted their bonds. What info was a lie…what info is valid!

I had one more question for DA Baxter…which, to me, was very important to help direct us in our investigation. So…I called him; Susie answered. She said he was out of the office but could she help me? Being the DA's right-hand lady, I'm sure she could! I asked her if she could check to see if there were any warrants issued for Sarah Vasquez, Rudolph, and Judith Jameson. She said she'd call me back in ten minutes.

If there were warrants for their arrest, they would be *laying low*, not wanting to bring attention to themselves…which may prove to be a little more difficult for us! But, then again, I have Darren and Steve, being my *skip-tracing* experts…they can find anyone!

Susie called back within five minutes. Yes, warrants were issued six months ago…the same time as the others…they just evaded law enforcement! The warrants were for $150,000 each…the same as Beaumont. I asked her if they had compiled any case info on them… did they have a file I could review…just to get some of their basic info? She said to come by at four, and she would give me what they had. It's nice to have friends in the DA's office!

Darren and Steve were already working the computers, Gina was still reviewing all the info in front of her, and Donny was talking with David. I told Steve and Darren I was picking up some more info on the Jamesons and Sarah Vasquez from the DA, which we needed to follow up on…this may provide us with clues regarding Beaumont's habits. The guys said they'll be at the computers for at least another two hours…just give it to them when I get back.

Seeing Donny hang up his phone, I walked over and gave him a shoulder hug! Looking up at me, he said David is flying down tomorrow morning, and he'll pick him up at the airport at ten thirty. Awesome! So he continued saying, "Let's call a meeting for 1:00 p.m. Everyone will have the night to review all this info, and we can start developing our initial plan of action." Works for me! While everyone was still in the conference room, he asked if they would be available for a meeting tomorrow, same time, so we can begin our investigative process. Everyone's on board. Plus, David will be here to throw in his two cents!

Time to pick up my info from Susie. Naturally, she has it ready for me when I get to her office. Three sets of papers, neatly paper-clipped together. Each set contained two pages, which detailed all the information the DA's office had compiled on these fugitives. This may prove to be quite helpful. I, again, thanked her for her help. All she said was, "No, the DA's office. Thank you!"

DA Bill Baxter and I go back many years! He knows I always get my man, which saves the taxpayers money. He doesn't have to assign his investigators to the case…knowing we will do everything possible to bring our fugitive to justice. With the cutbacks in the police force and the DA's office, he considers us an extension of his office. So, anything he can do to help us, he will do! And I always keep him posted on our progress…just to keep him in the loop!

When I got back to the office, Nelly was working with a new client, Darren and Steve were plugging away on the computer keyboards, and Gina and Donny were getting ready to leave. They wanted to get home, let all of this sink in…try to get their ducks lined up! Before they left, I made some copies of the papers Susie provided me and gave one to each of them…more food for thought! I then walked to the back of the office and gave Steve and Darren their copy…more *skip tracing* for them!

Not surprisingly, Marla got to the office early. She wanted to see what she could find out from the *friends and family* listed on the Beaumont bail application…how much was true…or not. She went into the investigator's office to make her calls…not wanting our new clients to hear her conversations. Good thinking, Marla!

I sat down at my desk…getting comfortable in my ratty chair! I pulled out my copy of the DA's info and studied it. Knowing this is just ancillary info on these *known associates*, we might happen to find some valuable tidbits that could eventually lead us to our fugitive.

Rudolph and Judith Jameson:

Rudolph: forty-three years of age; five feet eleven, 180 pounds

Five years ago, served eight months in county jail for identity theft

Address: local; also owns a home in Central California, valued at $1 million; owns a thirty-seven-foot sailboat, valued at $250,000, moored at Lost Point Marina, Southern California

Bank accounts: frozen

Employment history: real estate agent for seven years, various agencies. License canceled six months ago

Judith:

Forty-two years of age; five feet seven, 150 pounds

Employment history: administrative assistant at a local real estate Agency for three years

Both are charged with six counts of title fraud and one count of identity theft.

Knowing that Rudolph previously served some time in jail, we can get a copy of his booking photo and court file. At least we would have an idea of what he looks like. His case file may include some relevant info.

Sarah Vasquez:

Thirty-one years of age; five feet four, 118 pounds, long brown hair

Employment history: A *traveling notary*; independent contractor, not employed by any real estate agency; she travels with her notary seal and book to wherever she is needed. Her standard of living is dependent on the work she receives from the "Jameson Network."

"Good information…Thanks, Susie!" The tapping of the keyboards is coming from the conference room…Darren and Steve are still plugging away! I ask them to please take a look at the new info when they get a chance. There might be something we can use.

* * *

Marla has finished making her preliminary calls regarding both Beaumont and Campbell. She found there was definitely an overlap of friends listed on both apps! However, she did find one name on Beaumont's app that was not included on Campbell's: Brooke Marino, her hairstylist!

While Marla was finishing up her review, I jumped on my computer. Something had been bothering me: why didn't we catch the similarities between these two clients? I pulled up the app on Campbell first. We posted her bond five and a half months ago. Everything appeared just fine for the bond: cosignors, credit checks, the usual. Plus, their premium check cleared the bank. She made her first three court appearances, then decided it was time to get out of Dodge! Jump bail! It only took us a month to find her and return her to custody.

Next, I check our latest *skip*: Blake Beaumont. We posted her bond six months ago…before Campbell's! The charges were quite similar…but that happens all the time. It would be like posting bonds for people with similar drug charges. Nothing sounded the alarm at the time! The bail amounts weren't the same: Beaumont, $150,000; Campbell, $100,000.

I brought this info to Marla's attention. She's printing out the apps for both, highlighting the relevant info, and will make copies for the meeting.

Nelly was finishing up entering the info into the computer for her new clients. I asked her if she could make arrangements to pick up the booking photo of Rudolph Jameson, along with a copy of his previous court case. This may provide some insight into him and his partners in crime!

I checked the time…4:30 p.m…the court will be closing soon. So, Nelly, getting ready to call it a day, jumped up, grabbed her purse, and ran over to the court. As she's running out the door, I told her I would make the arrangements for the booking photo. She waved a *thumbs-up* gesture back.

I called up one of my deputy buddies at the jail and asked him if he could locate the booking photo for Jameson, which went back five years. He asked me to hold on while he checked the county computer. Within thirty seconds, he was back! He found it and would have a copy for me at the front desk in fifteen minutes. What a guy! I, naturally, thanked him.

On my way over to the jail, I texted Nelly I was on my way over to pick up the photo. She immediately replied the court clerk found the old case file in their computer system. She's trying to find the actual file now. And, if successful, will make copies for us! You never know what information you can find from old case files. A leopard doesn't change his spots!

Entering the jail, I see some more deputy buddies behind the front desk. One of them is holding up a brown envelope for me. After handing me the envelope, we all schmoozed a bit…still laughing over the failed *jailhouse wedding*!

Returning to the office, I stopped at our corner burger joint and grabbed some burgers and fries for Marla, myself, Darren, and Steve. She came in early to help, so I figured she might be hungry…I knew I was! While at the burger joint, I talked with my friend, the owner, and placed another lunch order for tomorrow at one o'clock…for eight people. He'll have it ready! This man takes good care of us…at least food-wise!

As Marla is printing out the info from our computer, she's making the copies we will need for tomorrow's meeting, and setting up the conference room. Nelly texted me that she was able to obtain the old case file, and she'd drop it off at the office on her way home. Perfect.

Coming out of the conference room, Marla spots the bag of burgers on my desk. As I finish making copies of the booking photo, I head to my desk. She's already sitting in *my* ratty desk chair, pulling out the burgers and fries. I take the food back to my guys…gotta keep them happy! Placing the photocopies on the desk, I pull up a chair, and in between bites, Marla and I start going over the info we have…making sure we have most of our ducks lined up for the meeting.

Halfway through our burgers, Nelly walks in with the copies of Jamesons' court case file. I told them both that I'd be in the office by 6:00 a.m…and I would really appreciate it if both of them could be present for the meeting. I really need their input and help. I told Marla to plan on leaving when I get in tomorrow morning… to get home and get some rest and, if she could, be back about twelve thirty…right before the meeting. I also asked Nelly if she would like to get in at eight thirty tomorrow morning. Let her catch an extra hour with her kids. They both said they'd think about it…we still had work to do!

Nelly grabbed some of my French fries. "For the road," she said, and left. Marla is enjoying our little break…still kicking back in my chair! Before I head home, there is one more thing I want to check out: Beaumont's hairstylist, Brooke Marino.

Darren and Steve were finishing up their skip tracing for the time being…printing out info as they came across it. I asked them to run one more name…Brooke Marino. Telling them she is listed on Beaumont's bail application, and she's local. We need to find out more about her and if she has any other type of connection to Beaumont, aside from hairstylist! They said they'd have the info tomorrow morning…and they'd be in the office by ten…they still have a lot of things to check out…like all social media platforms.

* * *

A few years back, the team was working a case…a $20,000 bond / $40,000 warrant: Ricky Latimer, twenty-three years old, drug charges. They ran their social media searches, skip tracing, and Internet checks. From that info, Darren developed a *friends and family tree.*

The cosignor/indemnitor on Ricky's bond was his sister, Rose Latimer. Both she and Ricky, according to his bail application, lived locally. But, naturally, since he *jumped bail,* his contact numbers had been disconnected…and he skipped out on the rent for his apartment. Rose wasn't much better. However, she still had her job at the dress shop listed on the bail app.

The team found Rose working at the shop. After interviewing her, she, of course, stated she hadn't seen her brother in over two weeks…and had no idea where he was. Yeah, right! The team reminded her of her $20,000 responsibility…she said if she hears from him, she'll call us!

We ain't stupid…we know how to do our job…she was lying, of course!

Well, Little Miss Rose and Ricky *love to post their lives on social media*…let the world know how important they are!

On one of the media platforms, Rose posted about an upcoming family reunion…how excited she was! The parents, aunts, uncles, cousins, brothers, and sisters would be attending. They were expecting over 150 family members. It was going to be so wonderful to see everyone again!

The reunion was to be held on Saturday, the 24th, at Lamont Park, from 10:00 a.m. to 4:00 p.m…and everyone was to bring their favorite dish…drinks would be provided!

So, we now have a date and location…this was too easy! Darren rounded up the team and filled them in on the *operation*. The 24th was only two days away.

Saturday, the 24th, rolled around. The team met up at the office at 9:00 a.m. Darren handed out copies of Ricky's booking photo. Having their plan of action in place, they drove to Lamont Park... only fifteen minutes away, getting there a little early, 9:40 a.m.

Upon their arrival, they could see people heading toward a specific area in the park with cement tables, benches, and built-in barbecues. This had to be the spot. Within minutes they see some men hanging a banner: "Welcome to the Latimer Family Reunion." Yep, this was the spot!

More people arrived, placed trays of food on the tables, set up a variety of games, and connected some sort of music system. Looks like it's going to be a fun family reunion.

Darren and the team, not wanting to disrupt the reunion, memorize Ricky's booking photo. They haven't seen him yet...and don't know when he will appear...let alone *if* he will show! Patience!

There are probably fifty-sixty people in the picnic area now... it's 11:00 a.m...more are expected. Still no sign of Ricky...but lots of time left.

The team takes turns getting out of their cars, so they can mingle with the family members...all the while looking for Ricky. First Gina, then Steve, next Darren, and lastly, Donny. No sight of him yet. By this time, it's 2:00 p.m...is he going to show up? Only two hours left for the reunion. The people are having fun, playing games, and enjoying each other's company...let alone all the food!

Gina decides to take another stroll pretending to mingle with the family...needing to stretch her legs. She comes across a small group of women just talking about their families. She hears the name "Rose" mentioned...and listens more intently.

Rose is telling the other ladies that Ricky just called her...saying he'd be there soon...he wanted to swing by and pick up his girlfriend. Gina headed right back to the team...telling them he's on his way and has a girlfriend with him. They again, look at the entrances to the park...only one. But once in the park, you have to go to the right or to the left to park.

They see some areas where they can hang out, still blending in...and waiting. In less than ten minutes, a car enters the park...it's

Ricky and his girlfriend. He turns to the right to find a place to park. Donny and Steve, on foot, are following him. Gina and Darren are easing their car to the location. Donny approaches Ricky's side of the car, and Steve maneuvers to the girlfriend's side.

Ricky gets out of the car, runs his hands over his clothes in an attempt to smooth out wrinkles, then shuts his door. As he starts walking toward the front of his car, Donny approaches him and introduces himself and Steve. As he is being arrested, Steve takes the car keys from his hand and gives them to the girlfriend.

Donny, quietly, places Ricky in the back of Gina's car and advises the girlfriend to go home.

Oh, one last thing, Gina allows Ricky to text his sister Rose to let her know something came up, and he won't make it to the reunion!

Social media…ain't it grand!

CHAPTER 6

Threading the Needle!

It's still dark when I arrive at the office...6:00 a.m...the roosters aren't even awake yet! Marla is straightening some papers on her desk. In addition to gathering the info on Miss Blake Beaumont, she met with two families and completed their paperwork. Now, we just need to drop the bonds off at the jail.

I kicked her out of the office and reminded her about our one o'clock meeting today. She said she'd get the bonds posted at the jail on her way home and definitely be back for the meeting. What would I do without her!

I was expecting Nelly in at eight thirty. The clients Marla is posting the bonds, for now, should be in the office by noon to complete their part of the bail application. Darren and Steve should be in at 10:00 to continue their skip-tracing endeavors. Donny, Gina, and David will be in at about 12:30 p.m.

So, I'm by myself for a couple of hours. My mind is swirling around...trying to think if we are lining up our ducks the way we should be! But I know we'll have more info after the meeting...and what direction we will need to take.

I look around the office to see if there's anything I need to do... nope! All is good. I do, however, see an empty coffeepot...well, I can handle that issue!

Sitting at my desk, I start jotting down notes and items I want to bring up at the meeting. As I complete my third page of notes, I hear the front door open and see Nelly walk in. It's only 8:00 a.m. She's early, as usual! But just in time for the fresh pot of coffee! We both grab a cup, sit at my desk, and discuss the events of the previous evening…and what to expect for the day. Clients that should be in about noon and the upcoming meeting…let alone *lunch*!

The morning is quite uneventful! Just normal business: scheduling appointments for potential clients and updating client information. Nelly volunteers to call the court to check on the status of some of our bonds…to see if they are cleared yet. Great idea. I jump on the computer to see if we have any delinquent accounts payable. Just a couple, but I know Marla, my bulldog, is on top of it.

Trying to get as much info ready for my team, prior to the meeting, I pulled up the jail website and started my search for Lisa Montgomery, Dean Caravello, and Samuel Peyton…the three members of the Gang of Eight that *did not get bailed out*. I wanted to see what the website could tell me about their charges and possible next court appearances. I also wanted to check the website for the current status of Christine Campbell, the lady we placed back into custody several days ago.

Montgomery, Caravello, and Peyton were still in custody, with a next court appearance scheduled in four days. Campbell's court appearance was set for the same date. This may be their sentencing date. They could each be looking at eight years in prison, plus restitution.

Amazing…Beaumont, Vasquez, and the Jamesons are running around free…and *they're* facing some serious prison time. If I was them, I wouldn't be too happy about this situation…and maybe they're not either!

Having some time on my hands, I called over to our corner burger joint to confirm our lunch order for twelve forty-five today… and asked if they could possibly deliver it for me. Not a problem. One less thing to worry about!

As I'm hanging up the phone, Darren and Steve walk in…no donuts though! Today is the day I could really use a donut or two… need that extra sugar rush! Oh well, I'll survive!

The guys greet Nelly, shoulder hug me, and walk directly back to the conference room. I hear them shuffling papers around on the table and then the whirring of the computers starting. They're getting right to work. I grabbed a pot of coffee and three cups and headed to the conference room. I needed my guys caffeinated!

After pouring us each a cup of coffee, I sat down with them, looking at the papers they had assembled on the table. They've accomplished a lot! I asked them if they were able to find anything on our hairstylist, Brooke Marino. Darren ruffled through the papers and found the information on Marino. She is a bona fide hairstylist, licensed by the State of California. She has no complaints against her business according to the Better Business Bureau. It appears her only connection with Blake Beaumont is client-based. She has been Beaumont's stylist for over three years. Marino seems to be a stand-out citizen in the community. The one item they did find was *she had purchased her home two years ago from Beaumont, at a greatly reduced price!* Roughly $80,000 under market value!

Wow! I wonder if she questioned this price reduction? I asked Steve if he could run over to the Hall of Records and get a copy of the deed and anything having to do with the mortgage. The Hall of Records is located next to the courthouse…so it shouldn't take too long. I think it may provide us with a little more information which could be vital for our investigation. After taking a sip of coffee, he's out the door and should be back within an hour.

Darren is looking at me with a big smile…he knows what I'm thinking! With any investigation, you need to know who all the players are…and what is their connection to everyone else. Who does what? Who knows what? Where is their primary base of operations? And that's to start the investigation. As we dig deeper, more info, naturally, is developed, which may lead us in other directions. But we have to start lining up our ducks as soon as possible…and get the dots connected! And I think we are headed in the right direction now!

He starts reviewing the info, all the printouts, that he and Steve came up with…*checking out his ducks*! He's arranging his info according to names in order to provide us with a succinct presentation. So professional!

The morning is actually flying by now! And, boy, is it fun! I love the game of cat and mouse! We always win…and how we get there is where all the excitement lays! We don't need any catnip to spur us on!

My stomach starts growling…I look at my watch…only 11:45 a.m. Have to wait an hour or so for lunch! Where's a donut when you need it! I notice the empty coffeepots…so, knowing my team should be getting in soon, I head over to the coffee stand and set up the coffee…should be done in five minutes.

Only one potential client was scheduled to come in this morning…they haven't arrived yet. So, Nelly is standing by…all ready for them. Hopefully they will be in soon. I really need Nelly in on our meeting.

While studying the three pages of notes I made earlier, I hear some boisterous laughing coming from outside my office. Out of curiosity, I get up and walk to the front door. I see three crazy people performing some type of hula dance on the sidewalk in front of my office. I burst out in laughter…it's Donny, David, and Gina! Evidently, David is telling Donny and Gina some stories about his recent *callouts* with his Northern California Police Division. He's relating the various antics which people perform in order to avoid being arrested! We've all seen these antics over the years! The running, the hiding, and trying to drive away to avoid capture…whatever they think can save them!

Nelly and I are getting our hugs as they all walk in…still laughing over David's stories. I haven't seen David for over a month…he still looks great…and Gina, with a big smile, appears to agree! While David is in town helping us, he'll be staying with Donny, his old friend.

After they each grab a cup of coffee, they head back to the conference room to get ready for the meeting. I followed them in and pointed to the stack of papers on the table and told them not to touch them…don't get nosy…all will be explained in due time! As we're in the conference room, I hear Steve come in, back from the Hall of Records. He heads to the copier, in a rush to make copies of the paperwork he picked up! Must be something good! I can hardly wait! He winks at me to acknowledge my thoughts were right on! I smile as he gives *only me* a copy so I can study it before the meeting. The ducks are still waddling but not quite so much!

Just about everyone is here…only missing Marla…and lunch. They should *both* be getting here shortly. While we're waiting, I ask David if Donny has brought him up to speed on our case…and did he have any thoughts. He said he is up-to-date but wants to hear what additional info we have before he puts out his thoughts. He is such a great addition to our team…our family! They are getting comfortable at the table, still telling their stories, each one trying to outdo the other regarding their comical apprehensions.

Looking somewhat refreshed, Marla arrives carrying a small stack of papers. I'm even curious about these! She hollers at me to meet her at my desk. I comply as she is handing me the papers. I look at them, thumbing my way through the pages. She points to quite a few entries in the papers…she's smiling now…and so am I. This info solidifies some of my thoughts.

When she left this morning to go home, she wanted to follow up on some information she found. So, she hit the recorder's office before she came in…to see if she was right. And she was! All she had to do was enter a name into the county's computer system, and any information associated with that name would pop up. What she was looking for was a listing of the properties sold in our county for the last three years…which would display the name of the real estate agent, mortgage lender, notary, and the real estate agency. Without saying anything else, she hurriedly made copies for everyone.

Marla's finishing up with her copies, the team is getting situated in the conference room…and lunch arrives. The best way to start off a meeting is with food! I set the boxes of food on the table, everyone grabs a sandwich and a bag of fries. I had previously set out bottles of water. Now we are ready to discuss the case!

I started off by drawing their attention to the jail website print-outs. We have four people in custody still…four of our Gang of

Eight! Two women, Christine Campbell and Lisa Montgomery. Two men, Dean Caravello and Samuel Peyton. I pointed out the fact that they should be getting sentenced in the next four days…looking at some serious jail time! Continuing, I said I would like to go to the jail and interview the women, and think Donny should interview the men.

These inmates, both men and women, know they will be heading to prison soon…so what do they have to lose in talking to us. They were essentially hung out to dry by their partners in crime… no one bailed them out! They can't be too happy about that! Donny and I need to see what else they can tell us about Blake Beaumont… and their whole operation! And we need to do it as soon as possible, hopefully tomorrow!

The team agreed. Next, Darren stood up, with papers in hand, and directed us to the website printouts on each individual he and Steve had compiled. "First was the information about Brooke Marino, Beaumont's hairstylist. Not much there. Ms. Marino advertised her business on various social media platforms…and has built a profitable business. Beaumont had been her client for the last three years, but she hasn't seen her for over four weeks. She is well respected in the community. The only other connection she had to Beaumont was the fact she purchased her home from her…for $80,000 under market value! But he said he'd circle back around to that issue later!

"Next: Sarah Vasquez. She is a traveling notary. Not working for any specific real estate agency, goes where she is needed. Her job within the Gang of Eight is to notarize their fraudulent documents and, if necessary, forge the necessary signatures. She does not own a house. Rents an apartment…which she has not been to for over five months. The apartment owners are currently preparing the eviction documents. She has one credit card…and the only recent charge was made six weeks ago for a train ticket to San Francisco."

Digging a little deeper, Darren found one hit on her credit report…one for an apartment rental in San Francisco…and we have the address! He was unable to find any active bank accounts, and she has not filed taxes for the last six years. "There is a chance she may be in the San Francisco area. But," he continued, "where is she getting her money? She had always relied on her income from doing jobs for the Gang of Eight." And they are no longer in operation… so we think!

"Please turn the page. Rudolph and Judith Jameson, husband and wife. They owned a house locally which was repossessed three months ago…due to nonpayment. More on that later. Rudolph had been a real estate agent for over seven years; however, his license was revoked six months ago when the charges of title theft and ID theft were levied against him. Judith has never been a real estate agent. She has been an administrative assistant for one of our local real estate agencies, giving her access to a variety of documents, let alone inside knowledge of homes that will be coming on the market. Rudolph was also listed, up to six months ago, as an associate at a mortgage lending company.

"A property search showed he and Judith owned a home in Northern California, valued at $850,000. He paid $400,000 in cash and took a mortgage out on the balance. According to the records, the mortgage is paid for the next six months. Question: could Sarah Vasquez and the Jamesons be running their scams in the San Francisco area? Food for thought."

A credit report showed he had three credit cards, which are still valid. Recent charges, from two months ago, revealed some hits in the Honolulu, Hawaii area. "The Jamesons," Darren continued, "also own a thirty-seven-foot sailboat, which is moored at our local marina. Need to check it out!"

"Jameson's specialty was conning people, using quitclaim deeds. Stealing property from some people and then selling it to others via the quitclaim deed process! The district attorney's office estimates they stole over seven homes in our county, for a total income of $5,250,000! And…one of these homes was sold to Brooke Marino, via Blake Beaumont!

"Last, but not least, Rudolph was in custody five years ago for identity theft. He served eight months. A copy of his old booking photo is attached to his pages. We were able to obtain a copy of his court file on this old case, but nothing is relevant…all info is out-dated. He is very good at what he does…stealing from other people!

It wouldn't surprise me if he was considered the mastermind of the *gang*!

"Please keep in mind, the Jamesons and Vasquez are not our concern. We have no money invested in them. However, I bet wherever they are…Beaumont won't be far behind. We have to check out all the crumbs and see where they lead us!

"Now, let's get to Blake Beaumont. She had been making her scheduled court appearances until recently. Seeing her sentencing date rapidly approaching, she decided to hit the road! Her job within the *gang* was to procure the *marks* with the assistance of Judith Jameson and Christine Campbell. They would all take turns in forging the necessary documents, with Sarah Vasquez sealing the deals as the notary. Please remember that Christine Campbell's mother, Caroline, is the cosignor for Beaumont's bail bond…where is Caroline? Need to follow up on her…especially since she will owe us money!"

Darren moved on to Christine Campbell. She and Beaumont have known each other for about four years. They had both a personal and professional relationship. Both were real estate agents. Christine was charged with embezzling money from the agency she worked for, over $100,000…and stealing blank mortgage documents, along with the agency's notary seal. We arrested her a couple of days ago at her mother's house, hiding in the trunk of her car. She is set to be sentenced real soon.

According to county records, she does not own any property. Her real estate license has been canceled. In addition to looking at some serious jail time, the district attorney will be hitting her with a restitution bill of over $1,000,000! You are probably asking: What did she do with all the money she made from her share of these scams? Well, after doing some more digging and getting creative, he remembered that Rudolph Jameson was arrested five years ago for identity theft! Hmmm!

Darren started switching the names around, mixing up the first names and the last names…just out of curiosity…it was a good place to start at least. Within minutes he found the name: *Christine Beaumont*! How nice she took her best friend's last name! Having this info in hand, he started his skip tracing for Christine Beaumont.

After conducting a new record's search, he discovered that "Christine" did own property in Waikiki, a condo, completely paid for in cash. The monthly home owner's association fees were $795…and were paid in advance for the next year! So, she doesn't have to worry about that expense…what a shame she won't be able to enjoy the sun and beach, now that she's locked up! This is great info. We now may be looking at another possible location for Blake Beaumont…Waikiki! And, remember, the Jamesons had several credit-card charges in the Honolulu area several months ago! We'll need to, naturally, follow up on that.

Darren, finished his presentation…whew! A lot to take in! He asked if anyone had any questions…they all shook their heads, while still highlighting the many high points!

Okay…so now it's Marla and Nelly who step up…and pass out their copies to the team. Nelly began stating that Steve had collected some information from the Records office earlier this morning… and Marla followed up on some thoughts she had…which were confirmed by the info *she* gathered from the Records office.

Nelly asked everyone to look at the paperwork associated with the deed of trust for Brooke Marino's property. "Do you notice anything in particular?" It's quiet only for a minute…then David explodes…"The real estate agent is Beaumont, the notary is Sarah Vasquez, and the mortgage company is the one Jameson is affiliated with! OMG!"

Next, Marla passes out her copies to the team…more deeds of trust…six in total! She asks them to quickly review the information on each one…"Do we see a pattern?"

Lots of comments, some not so nice, are coming from around the table! It appeared that Rudolph Jameson and Blake Beaumont would take turns representing themselves as the real estate agent on the documents. And Sarah Vasquez and Judith Jameson would alternate as the notaries. However, all of these quitclaim deeds were *mortgaged* through Rudolph Jameson!

From what we could determine, Judith Jameson, in her role as administrative assistant at the real estate agency, had insider knowledge of properties possibly coming on the market. She would notify her husband and Blake Beaumont of these property locations. Judith would begin assembling the necessary information, data, about the homeowners…information she obtained from the records of the real estate agency…essentially stealing their information. Then their plans were put into motion…stealing the properties and reselling them to unsuspecting buyers! The new buyers have no idea what will be coming their way! Marla adds that these six *stolen* homes were sold for way under market value…which probably made them attractive to the new buyers! The sales price for these homes totaled over $4,000,000! I wonder who got the money?

Looking out at my team, I could see the disgust on their faces! I asked them if they had any questions so far…still nothing. I reminded them that we only are concerned with apprehending Blake Beaumont. However, knowing what is going on with some of these other characters should help us in finding and arresting her.

I continued, laying out my initial plan of action: Donny and I would hit the jail tomorrow morning and interview Caravello, Peyton, Montgomery, and Campbell. I would like to have Darren and Steve try to locate Caroline Campbell, Christine's mother…she will owe us a lot of money! I also need them to check out the Last Point Marina, where the Jamesons have a boat moored. And because of David's familiarity with the Northern California area and his contacts, I would like him and Gina to follow up on the possible location in San Francisco for Vasquez…and anything that may pop up for the Jamesons. I mentioned if they were unable to find anything on the Jamesons, try mixing up the names…as Darren did with Campbell! Reminding them, Jameson steals identities!

In addition, I would call DA Baxter this afternoon and give him an update.

Everyone hung around for a couple of hours…going over the information…talking to each other. It was a great meeting…we have so much info to follow up on! Time to really get to work. Beaumont skipped out on her bail bond only a week ago…and we are now ready to release the hounds and put her back in custody!

I asked Donny if he could contact the jail to set up our appointments with the various inmates…starting at 8:30 a.m. He's on it.

While everyone is working on their *assignments*, I called DA Baxter. Susie answered and put me right through. He came on the line, asking me if we had her in custody yet! Smart aleck! Returning his question with some snarky comments, I started giving him my update. I started off with the possible location we developed for Sarah Vasquez: San Francisco. We are checking that out tomorrow and should have more for him at that time…then, he can decide how he would like to handle her…since she is not our responsibility! I also mentioned the Jamesons may be in the same area…and we're following that lead as well.

Now, coming to my gal, Beaumont. I told him she is a real piece of work! What a snake! But we have a feeling she may be in the Honolulu area. A lot of info is leading us in that direction! I further mentioned that Donny and I will be interviewing the remaining four members of the Gang of Eight, currently housed at the jail! I want to see what info they are willing to give up now, since they'll be heading off to prison soon!

Baxter was silent for a moment…taking it all in! He finally spoke up…saying what a fabulous job we have done so far…it was amazing! I asked him to please let us run with these leads and not bring in his investigators…I didn't want them scaring anyone away! In a rather serious voice, he commented that his investigators could not have developed the type of info we have…let alone in this short time frame! He added that if I need anything, just let him or Susie know…they were here for us! I told him I would keep him posted… especially on Vasquez tomorrow! Uncle Mike would be proud!

As I hang up the phone, Donny comes over to my desk and tells me we are all set for eight thirty tomorrow morning. We'll meet at the office at seven forty-five, do a quick review of things, and then head over to the jail. Works for me.

I left the team to discuss their plans. Marla still seemed some-what perky, having come in early, with little sleep the night before. I sat down with Nelly and Marla, with coffee in hand. I asked Marla if she was doing okay…she replied *naturally*! Nelly was planning on staying a little late to keep her company…and besides they had one family coming in at 6:00 p.m. to post bond on their daughter. I told Marla, that while Nelly is here, she should go catch a cat nap on the cot in the investigator's office. She looked at Nelly and me, then promptly rose and walked back to their office. Looking over her shoulder, she said to come get her in thirty minutes.

Getting ready to call it a day myself, I made my way back to the conference room and bid everyone a good night! "We all have a busy day tomorrow…and please keep Donny and me posted on your progress." My team was going to hang out for just a few more minutes, then call it a day, also.

CHAPTER 7

The Truth Shall Set Thee Free!

It's going to be a fun day…lots of stuff happening. It's six thirty in the morning. Marla is pretending to be perky, but I know she is dragging…it's been a very busy two days for her. I hear the music playing in the background and see a full pot of coffee on the burner. I ask her to give me a rundown of the night's activities and what we should expect for today. Then, I sent her home to get some well-deserved rest! No arguments from her. I can hold the office down until Nelly gets in…piece of cake!

Knowing that Donny will be in within the hour, I jot down a few questions for our inmates: (1) Do you know where Jameson, Vasquez, and Beaumont are? (2) Do you know of any additional property or assets they might own? (3) Do you think they would continue working their scam, possibly in another county or state?

Very simple and direct questions. However, we need to impress upon each of them how they were left holding the bag! Their cohorts didn't even try to have them bailed out! All they have done is take the money and abscond to parts unknown! Donny and I need to get them angry over their situation…if they aren't already!

While waiting for Donny, I poured a cup of coffee…really trying to focus on our job at hand! And there again, it's only a fact-finding mission…trying to glean a few nuggets that will eventually lead us to Beaumont!

Still in my reverie, Donny and David arrive *really* early…David smiling big-time! When they got back to Donny's house last night, David contacted some of his fellow officers at his police department in Northern California. He asked if they could, cautiously, check out the address *we found* for Sarah Vasquez in San Francisco. He explained the situation, her charges, and the $150,000 warrant. He advised them to only *confirm* she is at the location and get back to him as soon as possible. Further detailing it is the district attorney in Southern California that must determine how to proceed further… we just need to get him the information. His friends told him they would get right on it…and should have something for him in the morning.

Well…it's morning…and guess what? David's friends called him bright and early saying that after sitting at her location since midnight, they spotted her taking her dog for a walk early this morning. One of their undercover officers approached her from the opposite direction, and nonchalantly, bumped into her. After apologizing to her, he introduced himself…and she introduced herself as *Sarah Vasquez*. His friend continued the conversation for a while; however, before they parted, she gave him her cell phone number, hoping to meet up with him again!

David thanked his buddies for all their help…he really appreciated them dropping everything to help him out! One of his fellow officers said, "Hey, she's got a warrant…she's a fugitive…it's our job!" Dedication!

Bingo! We were right! I'll put a call into DA Baxter in a few minutes and give him the news…and he can take it from there! David mentioned Gina would be in shortly. They wanted to run searches for the Jamesons. He helped himself to the coffee and then headed back to the investigator's office.

Donny pulled up a chair at my desk. I showed him the list of questions I came up with earlier, emphasizing the tactic we need to take…get them angry about being left behind. We're both on the same page!

A little early still to head to the jail, so I called DA Baxter, hoping to catch him in the office early! Susie answered the call with a bright and cheery greeting. When I use the office line to place a call, the caller ID displays "D. J.'s Bail Bonds," so Susie knew it was me! After some morning banter, she told me he just got in and will put me right through. He jumped on the line, and I asked him if he was sitting down! He knew I had something for him! All he asks is "Vasquez?" I replied we have confirmation of her location in San Francisco. I detailed the events of the previous evening by the local police officers.

I, again, reminded him that I have no jurisdiction over her. That it's up to him to decide how to proceed from here. Even with the $150,000 warrant, does he want the San Francisco law enforcement agency to make the arrest or send his own officers…saving extradition problems?

He said I made his day! Great news! He will call the DA in San Francisco and bring him in on the situation. Common courtesy! I also told him we are working on gathering info on the Jamesons… and may have something for him in the next couple of days. Baxter said he will take it from here…but keep me in the loop! Further stating he owed us *all* a *big* dinner!

It's time to get to the jail. Donny and I gather up our IDs and notepads. As we are saying goodbye to Nelly, Gina walks in, with a little extra kick in her step! Nelly, Donny, and I look at each other, grinning! We know what has given her this added *kick*!

* * *

Getting to the jail, slightly early, we checked in with the front desk…showed our IDs, even though they know us…we *all* have to follow protocol! The deputy produced his visitor's sign-in sheet. We confirmed with him that I was to see inmates Lisa Montgomery and Christine Campbell; Donny was to see Samuel Peyton and Dean Caravello. The deputy completed the necessary paperwork and issued us our visitor badges.

We stepped over to the security station, placed everything in a basket, and then walked through the metal detection area. We are good to go. The women's section is to the left; the men's is to the right. Donny and I agreed to wait for one another in the reception area when we're finished.

I had asked to see Lisa Montgomery first. She was waiting for me in an interview room, specifically set up for bail agents and attorneys. The deputy opened the door and directed me to the table where Montgomery was seated. I immediately noticed her hands were shackled to the tabletop. She was no more than twenty-three years old. Dressed in the orange jumpsuit, she looked beaten, both physically and mentally…had lost a lot of weight during her six-month incarceration! Her face was drawn…with eyes revealing a defeated outlook.

I pulled out the chair and positioned myself directly across from her. I introduced myself, explaining that I had previously posted the bail on both Campbell and Beaumont…however, no one *ever* asked me to post a bond for *her*. I continued telling her it was the Jamesons who posted the bond for Campbell, and Campbell's mother posted the bond for Beaumont. But no one came forward for her or her other two companions.

With my introduction done, I explained the reason for my visit: did she know where Blake Beaumont could be? I see tears welling up in her sunken eyes! She straightens up in her chair and lets it all out! She had been so stupid…she trusted all those people. She said it felt good to have a job, she had been unemployed for over a year. When a position opened up within their organization, she jumped at it. She was the gofer! Ran the errands, filed paperwork with the county recorder's office, picked up the *special* documents from both Judy Jameson and Christine Campbell, and delivered them directly to either Rudy Jameson or Blake Beaumont. She had no idea what they were doing…and didn't want to know. She was thankful to have a job and a paycheck.

I asked her if she ever heard them discussing other properties they might personally own…or any other businesses they had an interest in. She overheard Christine bragging that she and Blake were thinking about purchasing some property in Hawaii…she thought it was a condo or townhouse…something like that…but she wasn't sure. She wasn't around the Jamesons much. She was basically a secretary, and they didn't fraternize with the lowly staff! Hesitating a moment, she looked intently at me and said she did hear some talk about boats…but couldn't remember in what context. She didn't see Blake much…she was always busy *taking care of business*. It seemed to her Blake was the brains behind the business. She and Rudy held a lot of private conferences…which she had no access to, naturally.

Total defeat now took over her whole being. She couldn't believe she let herself get pulled into their activities…she should have been smart enough to ask questions. And look at her now…facing prison time.

I thanked her for her help and candor! And if it made things easier for her, we are avidly pursuing Blake…maybe she'll get a chance to see her before she is sent to prison! And I almost forgot…I told her she will be having some more company very soon…Sarah Vasquez!

I got up and walked over to the door. The deputy opened it and closed it tightly behind me. One interview down…one to go: Christine Campbell!

The deputy led me to a room, two doors down, and opened the door for me. However, it was empty. He told me Campbell was on her way…should only be a couple of minutes…just have a seat! I thanked him. He walked out the door and closed it securely after him.

The door opposite of where I entered…opened. Campbell, shackled with hands in front of her, was led into the room. The deputy brought her to the table and fastened the shackles to the table-top…then exited the room.

I, again, introduced myself…stressing the point I was the one who posted the bail bond on her…and she decided to run…*leaving me to hold the bag*…which I didn't appreciate!

She slumped down in her chair. Now realizing who I was! She apologized for what she put me and my team through…she was scared…didn't want to go to prison! Not being so nice, I asked her how it felt to be left *holding the bag* for Blake and her other cohorts! Choking up a bit, she said she thought she and Blake were good friends! They did a lot of things together…even inviting her to the company's many holiday parties…introducing her to everyone. She'd even swing by the office to visit her.

Now, realizing all Blake was doing was scoping out the operation! Using her! But she admitted, she let herself be used…she didn't have many friends! It felt great to have someone like Blake, beautiful, educated, and smart, take an interest in her…she would have done anything for her! Which she did! She got involved, businesswise, with Blake three years ago…helping her work the many real estate deals! It didn't take her too long to figure out what she was doing…basically fraud…but she didn't say anything…just let it happen. Blake made sure to take care of her…she made a lot of money…and got used to it! She was able to buy her mother a house! She never had so much money…she had to do something with it.

Last year, she continued, she and Blake took a vacation to Waikiki and had a terrific time. Being real estate agents, they decided to check out properties while there…it might be a good place to buy a house or two…to enjoy the sun and beach!

I asked her if she bought any property in Waikiki. She said "no" because it was really expensive, and the monthly association fees were ridiculous! I contemplated telling her what I now knew…but thought, *What the heck*! Cocking my head to the left, I told her she did *sort of* own a nice condo in Waikiki! And it was paid for in cash, with the monthly fees paid through the next year! She looked at me funny…denied owning the property! I asked her if she happen to know a "Christine Beaumont!" She turned beet red…anger growing at a rapid pace! Blake! She actually did it!

Christine detailed how she and Blake met up with a real estate agent from Waikiki, at his office…maybe he could show them some listings. While at his office, she asked if he could show her copies of their loan documents, deeds of trust, everything. She told him she wanted to compare them against the ones she deals with…just to check out the similarities! After finishing the tour of the available homes, they returned to their hotel…and Blake showed her a set of documents…ones she stole from the real estate agent! Christine admitted she did nothing about it…Blake was her friend! So, she thought! Rudy must have provided her with a false ID and somehow arranged the purchase of that condo!

I needed to change the subject, to let her calm down a bit! Since she brought up his name, I asked her if she had any idea where Rudy and Judy were. She thought for a moment, evidently realizing how she had let herself be pulled into their fraudulent schemes...so stupid! She stated her contact with Rudy was limited...he primarily dealt with Blake on all levels. Between him and Blake, they accomplished everything they set out to do!

She remembered Rudy talking about his boat at the Last Point Marina...what a beauty it was! In addition to his boat, he has some type of property in Northern California...not sure exactly where... just up north somewhere. I asked her, next, about Judy Jameson... how does she figure into this scheme of things. Christine, laughed slightly, saying she is dumber than dumb! Judy does whatever Blake and Rudy tell her to do...no questions asked! She and I were the ones responsible for finding the *marks* and stealing company documents. Adding that the $100,000 she stole from the real estate agency was all her doing. She wanted the money! And it was just sitting in the safe!

I had one last question for her...but I had to appear concerned! Looking her in the eyes, I asked her if her mother has had a chance to visit her while she's been in jail. She smiled back at me, seeming to perk up a bit, and said her mother had been in yesterday. She was happy to see her and hoped to see her again before being sent to prison. "Oh, and why did your mother sign for the bail bond on Blake?" She said she knew she and Blake were good friends...and, besides, Rudy told her to!

I thanked her and wished her luck. The deputy saw me rise from the chair, opened the door as I approached, and, again, locked it securely after me.

I made my way to the front reception area and waited for Donny. Pulling out my notepad, I quickly jot down the info I got from both Montgomery and Campbell. One thing we know is that Caroline Campbell, Christine's mother, is still in the area!

As I'm waiting for Donny, my cell phone rings…it's DA Baxter. He wanted to let me know Vasquez is in custody…arrested by the San Francisco Police. They are holding her until his officers can arrive to transport her back down…which may be tomorrow. Before hanging up…he teased me about finding the Jamesons! I told him to sit tight! But I wanted to talk to him tomorrow…maybe we could meet for a quick breakfast. No problem…we'll meet at the corner burger joint at 7:00 a.m.

As I'm putting my cell phone back in my pocket, I see Donny making his way to me. We both head to the front desk and hand our visitor's badges to the deputy. We exit the jail and make the five-minute walk back to the office.

CHAPTER 8

When the Rubber Meets the Road!

As we are approaching the office, I see two people entering, the man holding the door open for the woman. Must be potential clients. Donny and I walk in behind them…providing a warm greeting and thanking them for coming in. I introduced myself as the owner, and if there is anything we can do to help, just let me know. Nelly stood up, shook their hands, and directed them to chairs at her desk.

Knowing this family is in good hands, Donny and I make our way to the conference room. My gosh…it's 10:30 a.m.! Donny and I were conducting our interviews for over two hours. The time went by so fast! But we did get some more information.

As we enter the conference room, we see, and hear, David and Gina, working at the computer. David is tapping away on the keyboard, and Gina is pointing out various items that appear on the screen. They look up from the computer as Donny and I are getting comfortable in our chairs.

After a few minutes of joking around, I begin the recap of my interviews. Lisa Montgomery is twenty-three years old. Basically a *runner* for the Gang of Eight! She would do whatever they told her to do, file documents with the Records office, and pick up paperwork from Christine Campbell and Judith Jameson. She would then deliver the paperwork to either Beaumont or Rudolph Jameson.

Swears she didn't know what was in the documents. She needed her job…so did whatever was necessary to keep it.

Next, Christine Campbell. She thought she and Blake were good friends. Now knows she was being used by Blake. Worked real estate deals with Blake for three years and made a lot of money. Christine bought the house her mother is now living in because she had to *invest* her money somewhere! Evidently, she and Beaumont vacationed in Waikiki recently, looked at property to possibly purchase…but didn't. She had no idea that Blake was using a fake name: Christine Beaumont!

When I mentioned this name, she got quite angry…admitting Blake had stolen some type of deed of trust paperwork from the real estate agent and must have had Rudy supply her with the forged documents she would need to purchase property. She further mentioned she and Judy were responsible for securing the *marks* and stealing the necessary documents from the real estate offices.

I asked her why her mother signed for Blake's bond…all she said was, "Rudy told her to!" And…her mother visited her *yesterday at the jail,* so she is still here, most likely at her house.

The team is making brief notes…hoping this info will lead us to Beaumont. Donny now took over the briefing. He explained that Samuel Peyton's job was to drive around neighborhoods and find homes that were "For Sale by Owner." When he would find them, he was to give the information and location to either Rudy or Blake. He didn't know what they did with the info. He occasionally was asked to pick up envelopes from Christine or Judy and deliver them to Blake. Peyton, only twenty-two years old, had a wild crush on Blake…and would do whatever she asked of him!

Donny went on to mention he was really a nice young man… just a shame he was taken in by these people…but, like Lisa, he needed the job and the money was great!

He continued, moving on to Dean Caravello. Donny got a look of disgust on his face. Caravello was the brains behind all of the identity theft issues. He was completely responsible for producing all the fake IDs and documents that were needed to steal the homes of other people! He met Rudy Jameson five years ago…served time in the same prison as Rudy…and they became close friends. When they were both released from custody, within a month of one another, they met up and hatched their current plan! A real sweetheart of a guy!

Donny asked him if he knew where Rudy currently was…he said he had no idea. But Donny knew he was lying! He put an end to the interview…he couldn't wait to get away from this scumbag! Donny went on to make a few more rather colorful comments about Mr. Caravello…ones that even made me blush!

We all started making comments about the interviews…primarily regarding Campbell and Caravello! We all concurred they are *not very nice people*!

Before taking a quick break, I told them DA Baxter had Sarah Vasquez arrested yesterday by the local police department, and she is on her way back now! Thanks, David…and please make sure to express our appreciation to your friends!

Needing to stretch our legs a bit, we headed to the coffeepot… we see a full pot of coffee on the burner. Nelly is our hero!

She informed me the family I met earlier had decided to post the bail for their son…a $35,000 bail…domestic violence charges! She had run the credit check on them, and all came back positive. They paid the full premium of $3,500…and the funds were good, according to the bank.

I told her we were taking a quick break, and that if she would like to run over to the jail and drop the bond off, I could handle the office. She needed a break, so decided to take me up on my offer. Picking up the bail bond from her desk, she headed out. She'd only be gone for ten to fifteen minutes.

Instead of reconvening our meeting in the conference room… and we had no clients in the office now, everyone grabbed a chair and circled around my desk.

Gina, a little excited, said she and David came up with some very interesting info about the Jamesons…but wanted to wait until we were all in the conference room. She said it was a lot of info and didn't want to be interrupted in case a client came in. Makes sense. So, everyone, just relax for a few more minutes.

I took this time to ask Donny if he had heard anything from Darren and Steve. Nothing yet. He'll give them a call and see if they have any news.

* * *

Nelly returned from the jail and started entering the new client file into the computer. The rest of us head back to the conference room.

We take our seats…and David and Gina huddle over some papers…getting them in order. Gina starts her side of the briefing. Initially, she and David reran searches on the Internet to see if anything was showing up. Nothing! Then they entered the names of Jameson, Beaumont, and Campbell…to see if anything appeared linking them together. The only item that surfaced was their mutual crime spree!

Next, they began interchanging names. They tried this name combo…that name combo. But nothing was showing in their record searches or from any of the Hall of Records offices. They decided to concentrate on the San Francisco area.

They finally hit pay dirt with a *name combo*, and once they had the name, they double-checked their Internet and record offices search. These people are really the scum of the earth!

The Jamesons have assumed the names of "Rudy and Judy Peyton!" Their search of the Records office in the San Francisco area, revealed the "Peytons" purchased a house one year ago, just south of San Francisco. The house was valued at $650,000, and paid for in cash… no mortgage was showing. Gina was able to obtain the address for this property.

David jumped in…really eager and excited to continue with the briefing! Gina handed him a piece of paper, which was really a website printout. Now that they had the names the Jamesons were using, David and Gina jumped onto some social media platforms… and injected the names of Rudy and Judy Peyton! It didn't take long until their inquiry led them to a web page for "R and J Financial!"

David had a copy of the web page…it was a beautiful page, depicting a number of homes in the background, each having a "For Sale" sign in front of them. The caption announced: "We Buy Homes!" "Please call us for an appointment at 408-555-4757… We can make your dreams come true!" At the bottom of the page was listed their company name: "R and J Financial" and pictures of "Rudy and Judy Jameson!" Great…now we know what they look like…they were never arrested so we couldn't get copies of booking photos…and their DMV photos were old!

Gina reminded us that the Jamesons had their real estate licenses canceled…now the only thing they could do is *buy homes*! So, their trusting clients thought! They just came up with another scam!

David, wanting to have some fun, decided to call the number listed on the web page. It was answered but by an answering service. When he stated the reason for his call, the voice, evidently a paid secretarial service, replied that the "Peytons" are out of the office for the next ten days. She can certainly take down his information, and they will contact him upon their return to the office. David told her he would call back in a couple of weeks.

We all sat around the table, shaking our heads…trying to take in the scope of this *criminal organization*. Gina handed me the address for the house the "Peytons" purchased. I wanted to get this to DA Baxter but was waiting on a little more information from Darren and Steve. The Jamesons may not be *home* right now, according to the secretarial service.

It was pretty quiet in the front office, so Nelly came back and sat with us. Gina brought her up to date on the latest information. She couldn't believe the extent people go to in order to steal other people's property! If they would only put their efforts toward lawful endeavors…get an honest job like everyone else! But, alas, they are… and always will be, criminals…they know nothing else!

Donny is waiting to hear from Darren and Steve. I'm at my desk, making a few notes. I look up at the clock on the wall…one thirty…where has the day gone! David and Gina walk out of the conference room and tell us they have an errand to run…they'd be back in a few minutes. Nelly is just hanging out with me and Donny... still trying to take it all in!

While Donny is sifting through the pages of info we've accumulated over the last couple of days, he finally gets his call from Darren. He places his cell phone on speaker so Nelly and I can also hear, and grabs a notepad.

Darren placed his phone on speaker as well so Steve could chime in on the conversation.

So, here's the scoop! They started off their morning at the Last Point Marina, where Jameson keeps his thirty-seven-foot sailboat. They wanted to talk to the harbormaster...but he wasn't in yet. So, having Jameson's slip number, made their way to Jameson's boat slip...but it was empty. He and Steve looked around to make sure they were at the right location...they were! Steve spotted some people climbing out of their small sailboat, five slips down from Jamesons. Steve approached them carefully; it was still pretty early in the morning. He asked the couple if they knew Mr. Jameson. The couple said they knew of him and had spoken to him briefly, just to be neighborly! They said he didn't mingle with the other boat owners. When Jameson and his wife were on their boat, they stayed pretty much to themselves. The couple said they invited them on several occasions to join in on the Saturday night dock parties...but they never did!

Steve joined in on the conversation, stating the couple hasn't seen them for maybe two months...and about a month ago, they saw *someone else* taking their boat out...and it hasn't returned. The couple suggested we talk with the harbormaster. We told them we were just waiting for him to come in. We thanked them and told them to have a nice day!

Darren took back over now. The harbormaster finally made it in. They asked him if he had a second to talk. He said to give him five minutes...he needed to check his calendar for the day's activities...and his answering machine for any important messages that may have come in last night.

Darren and Steve made themselves comfortable in some chairs and waited for him. After *ten* minutes, he appeared with a smile on his face...nothing disastrous happened overnight! Darren and Steve identified themselves and showed him the warrant for Rudolph and Judith Jameson. The harbormaster's face turned ashen white…he was in total shock. Recovering his composure, he said they were such nice people…very friendly…got along with everyone! Which was completely contrary to what the nice couple had told them!

Steve told him they walked down to Jamesons slip and saw it was empty…what happened. He went on to explain the harbormaster said the Jamesons had sold their slip about a month ago and had hired someone to move it to another marina. Darren asked him if he knew which marina. The harbormaster asked them to wait a minute…he had some paperwork, signed by the person authorized by Mr. Jameson to relocate his boat. He returned, waving a piece of paper, showing the boat was assigned to a Captain Jake Carlson, to transport, or sail, the boat to Waikiki Yacht Club, Ala Wai Harbor, Waikiki, Hawaii. He seemed so proud of himself…that he had this paperwork! Steve asked him for a copy…no problem.

Donny cut in…telling them great job. This was good info that helps us hone in on Beaumont. We are getting more information which is pointing us in the direction of Waikiki. Donny then asks them about Mrs. Caroline Campbell…anything new on her? Steve told us they went directly from the marina to Mrs. Campbell's location…have been sitting on it for several hours…but not seeing any activity or movement. Steve said they want to watch it for a couple more hours…and if nothing happens, they'll proceed in talking with the neighbors.

But that's all they had for now. He and Darren will keep us posted if anything happens.

* * *

As Nelly, Donny, and I are still trying to process all the information, David and Gina walk into the office…backward…trying to hide what they are carrying. They're attempting to do *the moonwalk* back to the conference room! But it doesn't help…the smell of pepperoni pizza tells on them!

We all start laughing. I run to the kitchen area and grab some paper plates and napkins…what a great idea they had…and so thoughtful.

We're huddling around the four boxes of pizza…sausage, pepperoni, chicken, and bell pepper. After making our selections, we get comfortable around the table…ready to relax for a while.

While munching away, everyone is still throwing in their two cents about the case…what direction should we take next? What are we going to do about the Jamesons? The expression on David's face changes…he appears to be getting angry…and we all notice…Gina especially is baffled over this abrupt change in his demeanor!

Then…David bursts out laughing! He was just messing with us…but if they *really* want to hear a crazy story…he's got one that will outdo everyone else!

We're all kicking back in our chairs…relaxing…as David begins his story. About two years ago, he wanted to buy a relatively new *used* truck…he needed to keep up his *macho* image! Some of his fellow officers told him about a social media website that lets people post items they had for sale: appliances, furniture, sports equipment, clothes, cars, and trucks…at extremely discounted prices. Well, David thought he would check it out.

He found the website, saw the various categories, *clicked* on the button for cars and trucks…and started browsing the hundreds of vehicles listed. He was hoping to find a listing for a 2020 Ford 150 truck…or something close to it! David found twenty trucks listed. He *clicked* on the listing for each one…some were pretty beat up, some showed damage, and ten were older models…but there were a couple that looked okay. He was hoping to find a dark-blue truck… and there it was…and it looked in good condition.

The owner advertised the truck was in excellent mechanical condition, with no accidents, and he was directed to call for an appointment to check it out. David *clicked* on the picture to get a larger image of the truck…yeah, it looked to be acceptable. So he called the number and spoke to the owner…seemed to be a nice man. They set an appointment for nine the next morning. David got the man's name, Lyle Fenway, and his address. He also asked him for the vehicle's license plate number…which the man provided. Mr. Fenway said the truck is in perfect condition…just like driving it off the showroom floor. He also confided he needed to sell it because he was moving out of state and had an SUV, which was all he really needed. David said he'd see him in the morning and was excited about the truck.

After being in law enforcement these many years, David knew nothing is really as it seems…so he checked out the man…the vehicle…just to make sure nothing *hinky* was going on…and that the man actually owned the truck.

Still in his office at the police station, he entered the man's name and address into their database system. Immediately, a *red flag* popped up on the screen next to the man's name…with a notation to "contact the FBI if you have any information on this fugitive. Please contact Special Agent Gilroy at 408-555-8812."

So David calls Gilroy and identifies himself as a police officer with the local law enforcement agency. David explains the reason for his call…and that he is set to meet him tomorrow morning to look at a truck he has for sale. Gilroy told David the name the man gave him is an alias…his real name is Walter Conroy. He was wanted on a $1,000,000 warrant for manufacturing and selling drugs across state lines…California, Arizona, Nevada, and New Mexico! Gilroy further mentioned the man has been on the run for the last five years. He, and his associates, have been selling drugs to kids…and, unfortunately, four deaths are attributed to his drugs.

David, now having this horrible information, wanted to run right over and arrest him! But Gilroy asked him to keep his appointment with him. They wanted to arrest him at his house, and hopefully, shut down his drug manufacturing business! David realized the importance of this…and was amazed at how stupid this man was to post something on the Internet!

Gilroy told David he would have his team set up early at the man's house, not wanting to afford him an avenue of escape. If David would just keep his nine o'clock appointment.

Continuing his story, David tells them he arrived at nine as scheduled. He could see the undercover FBI agents in place around the house. The "Truck for Sale" was parked on the street…and it was a beauty!

The man evidently saw David approaching his front door and met him outside on the porch…not wanting David inside his house! David greeted him, making comments about how great the truck looked. The man mentioned his job is taking him to Arizona, and he won't be able to take the truck with him…so he decided to sell it.

He and David get to the truck, David walks around it, pretending to inspect it for possible damage to the body and framework. The man is standing on the sidewalk, holding the keys out to David…so he could start up the engine.

Within seconds, the FBI agents appeared and had the man on the ground and *cuffed*. The man was startled at first…then looked worried as he saw the agents entering his home. In the blink of an eye, the agents had him whisked off to parts unknown! And David saw the agents carrying out a myriad of equipment from inside the house! Boxes upon boxes of what appeared to be paperwork.

Agent Gilroy shook David's hand and thanked him for working with them. They have all saved the lives of hundreds of children!

David walked back to his car and was very happy they got this predator off the street…*but*…*he really wanted that truck*! Guess it's back to checking out what else is on the media website…one never knows what…*or who*…you'll find!

We were all listening to David's story in awe and disbelief! Still munching away on the pizza, David forgot to mention Gilroy called him later that week and reported they were able to take down…close up…one of the largest drug manufacturing rings on the West Coast!

Okay…we agreed…David won *the craziest story* competition!

CHAPTER 9

Will Wonders Never Cease?

The team is still hanging out in the conference room, trying to do more damage to the pizza…but I think there's going to be plenty left over to munch on tomorrow. And Marla will get a chance tonight to indulge and enjoy it!

Nelly and I are getting situated at our desks…she's reviewing the list of potential clients still scheduled to come in…I'm going through the last two days of mail. Don't see anything that needs my immediate attention…thank goodness!

I look up and see John, our mailman, walk in with a large envelope in his hand. He walks right back to me, hands me the envelope, and has me sign for it. A certified envelope from Uncle Mike in Florida! What is this all about?

I open the outer envelope and there is a smaller eleven-by-fourteen-inch package inside. On the outside of this envelope, Uncle Mike wrote on it: Do *not* open until I tell you to!

What is he up to? My curiosity is taking over, so, naturally, I call Uncle Mike! He's laughing as he answers the phone…he knew I'd be calling! I told him I just got his *envelope*! What's this all about? How come I have to wait to open it? He tells me to put it in a safe place for now. Also, saying he's planning a trip out next week to spend some time with me…should be out in five days! I tell him I'm so excited…I haven't seen him for a year…the staff will be thrilled to see him also! And he cautions me again…*do not open that envelope until he tells me to*! I promised I wouldn't…it will take all my strength not to! So I'll place the envelope in the safe…away from my curious hands!

I asked him if he wanted to stay at my place…got plenty of room. He said he'll just get a hotel room…he had some business to take care of while here and didn't want to interfere with my schedule.

This is great news…I let everyone know Uncle Mike will be here within the week…we need to plan something fun for him. Nelly volunteers to come up with something! She has three kids…and can be very creative once she is in her *party mode*! Full faith and confidence in Nelly.

I decided to call it a day…have a busy day tomorrow. I reminded Donny I'm meeting Bill Baxter for breakfast…and mentioned to him what I was thinking…did he think I should? He smiled and looked me in the eyes, totally agreeing.

* * *

I decided not to go to the office first thing this morning…I had my early breakfast with DA Bill Baxter. I called Marla to let her know I'd be in after…and did she want me to pick her up some breakfast? She said, thanks, but "no," she'd been eating leftover pizza all night! I had to laugh…I knew she would…she *loves* pizza!

Bill and I arrived at our café at the same time…getting my usual bear hug from him! We grabbed a booth in the back and placed our order. He started in by giving me a brief rundown on the status of Sarah Vasquez. She was booked into jail yesterday and will be taken to court this morning. Now, he looked at me…it was my turn!

I gave him my update on the Jamesons…and slipped him the address and phone number they are currently using. I told him about their latest *scam*: "R and J Financial!" I gave him a copy of their website ad. He looked at it, shook his head, then smiled. I continued telling him I didn't think they were there…according to their secretarial service. All the crumbs are pointing to the Waikiki area. I further mentioned the info Darren and Steve discovered at the marina, where Jameson kept his boat…which now may be on its way to Waikiki, getting confirmation from the harbormaster.

Bill was listening to every word I said…even jotting down notes. I went on to say I think he is meeting up with Blake Beaumont in Waikiki. Beaumont has spent some time there, even stolen real estate documents from a local agency. I think they plan on hatching a new scam! Almost forgetting some important info, she is now using the name of "Christine Beaumont!" Evidently, Dean Caravello made a new identity for her.

He agreed with my thinking and conclusions. Now, I told him, the main reason for wanting to get together: I wanted to discuss Lisa Montgomery and Samuel Peyton.

You know Donny and I met with them yesterday morning… talked with them for over an hour. They each explained their job within the company…which was just being runners. They'd pick up papers from Campbell and deliver them to Beaumont and Jameson. They were merely *gofers*…doing as they were told. They both needed their jobs and the pay was great, admitting they didn't know what they were involved in. They weren't allowed to open *any* of the envelopes they had to deliver to the others.

Peyton and Montgomery are young…twenty-two and twenty-three years old, naïve…and maybe a little stupid. Certainly not the brains of the operation!

Smiling ever so sweetly at Bill, I asked him if he could possibly have one of his assistant DA's re-interview them, along with their own attorneys present.

I was being honest with Bill…Campbell and Caravello were in this up to their necks…especially Caravello! I asked him if he knew that Caravello was the one providing all the forged and fraudulent documents for Jameson and Beaumont…let alone all the fake IDs?

Bill was still listening intently…still jotting down notes. I asked him if he could possibly review the cases on Montgomery and Peyton…they don't deserve the same sentence as Campbell and the others. It was Jameson, Campbell, Beaumont, Vasquez, and Caravello who deserve to rot behind bars for what they did to other hardworking, innocent people…not Peyton and Montgomery!

Taking the last bite of his omelet, he said he'd look into it right away because they have their sentencing date coming up in a couple of days. He said I was right to bring this to his attention…what's right is right! That's what our justice system is all about!

He looked at his watch, got up, gave me a quick kiss on the cheek, and told me he'd give me a call this afternoon…which I knew he would!

It was only eight five in the morning. Nelly had arrived at the office and got her morning update before Marla took off. Marla tells me she completed the paperwork on two new clients, even had a chance to run the bonds over to the jail…but hasn't had a chance to enter the new client info into the computer yet. She added the new clients should be in by noon to complete their end of the bail application. Well done! Nelly and I can handle the rest.

As I'm walking to my desk, I hear a booming voice coming from the conference room: where're the donuts? Donny, Darren, and Steve stepped out of the room…Steve finishing up the last of the pizza!

Next door to our bail office is housed a *really* vital component necessary to the well-being of me and my staff! "Dee Dee's Donuts." We have always supported her…even if she adds a few inches to our waistlines! The staff and I have known her for over ten years, since she took over the shop from her parents. Such a sweet lady! And her donuts are absolutely delicious!

I asked the guys if they wanted to go grab some donuts and coffee at Dee Dee's. Sounds good to them. We all walk over and find a booth. Dee Dee sees us and brings over four cups of coffee and some of her specialty donuts. "Meant for only her favorite customers." Guess that means us!

We're all eyeing the selection of donuts, and Darren dives in to make the first selection…the biggest bear claw you have ever seen! I'm sipping my coffee, trying to restrain from snatching up a chocolate éclair! Dee Dee comes over to the table and gives the guys her famous double-shoulder hugs! We haven't seen her for a couple of days…and she's missed us! After engaging in the usual banter, she slowly tells us she is *retiring*! Saying she decided it's time to see the world! And she wants to travel while she can still enjoy it! You could have knocked me over with a feather! She has been an institution in this community forever!

Recovering from our shock, Donny asks her if she is selling the business. She, coyly, says she is considering a couple of options… which should be decided upon in the next week! As she starts to turn away, looking over her shoulder at us…she declares there'll be the biggest party ever! Really need to celebrate!

The guys and I expressed our happiness for her…and tell her how much we will miss her…and her donuts!

Still trying to get over the fate of our favorite donut shop, Steve begins laying out the info he and Darren developed on Caroline Campbell. They sat at her house for most of the day yesterday and didn't see her. About five in the afternoon they decided it was time to talk with the neighbors. They first talked to the neighbor directly across the street from Caroline…a Mr. Barnaby. He said he knew her, saw her around but didn't really interact with her. He would wave at her if he saw her in the front yard…but that was about it. He also mentioned he did see her car in the driveway maybe two days ago.

Next, they met with the neighbor to the right. A Mr. and Mrs. Rafferty. A young couple, probably in their mid-thirties, with two kids and two dogs. Mrs. Rafferty, while trying to control her kids, said she was somewhat friendly with Caroline. And…what a shame it was about her daughter! She mentioned that Caroline was very proud of her daughter and what she had accomplished! Did we know that her daughter bought the house for Caroline? That was such a nice thing to do for her mother! We asked her when she last saw her. She glanced toward Caroline's house and said it had to have been two days ago because she was taking her kids to a movie. Caroline was in her front yard watering the flowers and waved at them.

Moving on to the neighbor on the left. A Mrs. Ellis, eighty-two years old. Darren thought she was probably the busybody of the neighborhood! We introduced ourselves to Mrs. Ellis, who then introduced herself as the president of the neighborhood watch! We asked her if she knew Caroline. She replied, "Certainly!" She knows everyone on the block…she even writes down the license plate numbers of cars that cruise around…stressing the point you just never know who is out there and what they have in mind! Better to be safe than sorry! We asked her when was the last time she saw Caroline. Without a moment's hesitation, she said, "Real early yesterday morning, about seven." She was loading several bags of luggage into the trunk of her car.

We asked her if she ever met her daughter, Christine. Nodding her head, she said yes, several times. Then added, looking directly at us, "It goes to prove what I've been saying for years. You never know who your neighbors are. You have to constantly be on your toes!"

Finishing up our coffee, Dee Dee brings over a box and places the remaining four donuts in it…Nelly will thank us!

So…we know a little more about Caroline Campbell: she's probably still around, and she was seen loading luggage into her car several days ago. We all discuss some potential scenarios; she's waiting around until her daughter is sentenced in two days, and she may be preparing to leave town after that. If so, where? Does she know where Blake Beaumont is? Is she going to Waikiki to join Beaumont, especially since she cosigned for her bail?

We need to find her…she will owe us money!

The guys and I wave goodbye to Dee Dee, and we all throw her a kiss. I'm carrying the donut box to the office…Darren and Steve take off, wanting to watch Caroline's house for a while longer. Besides, as Steve mentioned, they can run their skip tracing from the car. They're curious to see if she has used her credit cards recently… maybe purchased an airline ticket!

As Donny's leaving, he tells me we need to schedule a meeting with everyone…to start getting our ducks lined up…see where we are and where we need to go next. I agreed and decided two would be a good time. He said he'd let everyone know.

* * *

I'm back at my desk now…thinking about my team…my family…and how lucky I am! Hearing Nelly picking through the donut box, I remembered to tell her about Dee Dee…she's retiring soon!

We started reminiscing about the years past and what an impact she has had on all our lives…and the community!

The song "We Are Family" interrupts our conversation…it's my cell phone! It's the special ringtone I have set up for Uncle Mike! I quickly answer…very excited to talk with him and see him soon! He tells me there is a change of plans…he'll be arriving in two days… not five! Wonderful…all the better! I briefly laid out the case we are currently working on and asked him if he would like to help out if he had time. He said he'd love to and can't wait to see everyone. Besides, *I want to see what is in the envelope*! He gave me his flight arrival time, hotel, and rental car info. I asked him to call me once he was situated at his hotel. No problem!

I looked at Nelly…told her Uncle Mike moved up his schedule and will be here in a couple of days! Now we need to really work on coming up with something special for him…our time frame has been cut in half! With a devilish look on her face, she said it's all under control…just have to make a few adjustments, timewise!

She refused to tell me what she had up her sleeve…even though I promised her a raise, a new car, a bonus! But she wouldn't budge! Oh, well, I guess I'll have to be surprised just like Uncle Mike!

Still at my desk, I look up and see two people enter the office. They introduced themselves; he was one of our new clients Marla had posted the bail on last night! We had one other new client need-ing to come in as well. Nelly introduced herself and pointed to the chairs in front of her desk. She'll finish up his paperwork.

According to Nelly, Marla had made appointments with three other potential clients for this afternoon. Great…we need to keep our machine running! And Marla had even printed out their *jail* information before she left. That's my gal. I thought about calling her and telling her about our two o'clock meeting but then decided she needed her rest. We can fill her in later.

I spent the next twenty minutes going over some notes, getting myself ready for the meeting…and…thinking about Uncle Mike! He's up to something…I just knew it!

Now I'm hearing the song "Bad Boys!" I laughed to myself… this is the ringtone I set up for DA Bill Baxter. "Bad Boys…Bad

Boys…whatcha gonna do when they come for you!" With clients in the office, I stepped into the conference room to take his call. He's fast…I just left him five hours ago! Anxious to hear what he has to tell me!

Bill tells me he had one of his assistants meet with Montgomery and Peyton four hours ago…along with their attorneys. Long story short, he came to the same conclusion as we did…they were insignificant cogs in the overall fraud operation! They have been in custody for over six months. So, along with their attorneys, they agreed on "time served and three years' probation!"

"They should be released from custody tomorrow after their sentencing hearing." I let out a big sigh of relief. "However," Bill continued, "now that they have more info against Campbell and Caravello, they will be amending their complaint against them… adding additional charges. His assistant is supposed to meet with their attorneys tomorrow…and they could be facing up to fifteen years in prison!"

Before I had a chance to thank him, he also said he is amending the complaint and charges against Beaumont and the Jamesons! *He thanked me* for bringing this to his attention. Justice will now be served properly!

As I'm finishing up my conversation with Bill, David and Gina quietly enter the conference room…seeing me on the phone. Before hanging up, I told him Uncle Mike is arriving in two days, and I know he would love to see him! Bill said to definitely count him in…it's been a while since he has seen Mike! I mentioned I may have more on the Jamesons…but will call him tomorrow if we get anything new.

David and Gina jumped on the computer, still searching for more info on the Jamesons. I winked at them, saying we just received some good information, which I'll tell everyone about in the meeting. Darren and Steve walked into the room, carrying their briefcases.

Nelly was busy upfront, finishing up with the second family… and one family waiting patiently to bail out their son. Needless to say, she won't be joining us at the meeting.

Donny finally arrived and handed David some papers, looked like website printouts! David looked up at him and started laughing…Donny found him a dark-blue Ford 150 truck on the Internet! He thought David might be interested in making an appointment… adding he had already checked the owner out…the truck is not stolen nor is the owner a wanted felon!

So let's get started. I detailed what we knew: Beaumont could be using the name "Christine Beaumont." She stole real estate documents relating to property in Hawaii. She may be in the Waikiki area…and possibly purchased a condo under the name of "Christine Beaumont." Need to check it out…she may be there.

The Jamesons are using the name of "Peyton." They have established a new scam of "R and J Financial," running it out of the San Francisco area. However, they are not there now. Darren and Steve discovered recent credit card charges from restaurants in Waikiki and Honolulu, as recently as two months ago. Their sailboat is now on its way to Waikiki Yacht Club.

Do we feel the Jamesons and Beaumont are planning to meet somewhere in Hawaii to start their financial and real estate scams again?

These are questions we need answers to…answers that will start pointing us in a proper direction. Darren and Steve took over the briefing. Smiling, Darren told us he and Steve found Caroline Campbell at her house three hours ago! She confirmed she was waiting for her daughter to be sentenced tomorrow…then she is taking a short trip to Vegas to get away from things here. She is very disgusted and ashamed about what her daughter did. When asked about Blake Beaumont, she promptly spits on the sidewalk! Caroline said she is to blame for everything that has happened to her daughter…and wished nothing but the worst for her! And, no, she has no idea where she is…if she did, she would be screaming it from the rooftops! She knows she will be owing us money and is planning on selling her Mercedes to cover the bill. Before saying goodbye to Caroline, we confirmed her cell phone number and any other contact information.

Gina now jumped into the conversation. She and David may have found some property in Honolulu that is in the name of "Rudy

Peyton." They are waiting on confirmation. They have fake IDs… driver's licenses, social security cards, and passports. Everything necessary for purchasing real estate! She and David just finished talking with the harbormaster at the Waikiki Yacht Club. He confirmed a "Mr. and Mrs. Rudy Peyton" recently rented a slip at his marina, and their sailboat is scheduled to arrive in two days. A Captain Carlson called in yesterday to confirm the arrival date.

So we have a pretty good idea where the Jamesons are…or soon will be! And I bet you $1,000 Blake Beaumont will be there, too!

Steve was jumping up and down in his chair! While he and Darren were waiting for Caroline to show up this morning, he ran some more credit searches…plugging in the names of "Rudolph Peyton" and "Judy Peyton." They came across an American Express card, issued one year ago, in the name of "Rudy Peyton!" Further checking into this card, it showed two airline tickets were purchased ten days ago…tickets to Honolulu! So, we have some pretty solid info they are, indeed, headed to Honolulu/Waikiki!

Well…it looks like we are going to Hawaii! We have, so far, three locations to check out: the "Peyton" condo, the "Beaumont" condo, and the Waikiki Yacht Club Marina.

I remind everyone, again, we have no jurisdiction over the Jamesons…only Beaumont. I'll call DA Baxter and bring him up to date. We will most likely have to have the local law enforcement make the arrest on the Jamesons…however, Beaumont is *ours*!

We know the Jamesons/Peytons bought plane tickets ten days ago to Honolulu…and they are probably there now…and their sailboat should be docking in a couple of days.

Now that I'm thinking about it, I ask Steve, "Aren't boats registered with the DMV?" Let's check really quick and see if "Christine Beaumont" has a boat in *that* name. It's a possibility! Steve jumps on the computer…his fingers flying over the keys. Well, I'll be! Your right! The Hawaii DMV shows a fifty-five-foot houseboat registered to Beaumont!

I asked David to call the harbormaster at the Yacht Club and see if she has a slip there…it's a fifty-five-foot boat, a biggie, so I'm sure he'll know all about it!

David, really excited, grabs his cell phone and places the call. We're all listening in! The harbormaster, according to the receptionist, is out of the office, but the assistant harbormaster can help. He gets on the line and confirms her slip; she has had it for the last nine months!

Okay…now we have four locations to check out!

I could see Gina becoming a little agitated. She stood and walked around the room, swinging her arms in an attempt to relieve some of her tension. We're all watching her…feeling the same way!

She sits back down and apologizes, saying these people disgust her to the *nth degree*! They stole money from hardworking people so they could *live the high life* in Hawaii! We need to get these people! Gina, then asks us all a question: "If these properties, assets, were purchased with stolen money…ill-gotten gains…couldn't the government seize them?" We're all looking at her…we should have thought about that earlier!

I let everyone know I'll get with DA Baxter and see what he can do if anything.

Meanwhile, David, Darren, and Steve, can you get me the address of the Jameson/Peyton house in San Francisco and the registration numbers for both Beaumont's and Jameson's boats? Darren said to give them ten minutes!

While the guys are working on that task, I mention to everyone my conversation with Bill Baxter. Montgomery and Peyton will be sentenced to "time served and three years' probation" and released tomorrow after their hearing. And DA Baxter has filed additional charges on Caravello, Vasquez, and Campbell. They will now be looking at serving fifteen years behind bars…as opposed to the original eight years. And…he is also amending the complaint against Beaumont and the Jamesons.

The team was thrilled! Good for Bill Baxter. As Bill said previously, "Justice will now be served!"

Steve and David are feverishly writing on their notepads. They hand me the info on Beaumont and Jameson…great job! I'll call Bill and give him this new information.

Donny has been pretty quiet…I could see the wheels turning in his brain! He had been taking notes throughout the meeting.

"Okay," he blurted out! This is what he suggested doing: we need two teams to travel to Waikiki. David and Gina, one team… Steve and Donny are the other. We need to hit these locations at the same time, not giving them a chance to contact the other. However, we need to confirm they are there before we act. We'll need one day to check out the locations.

David and Gina will check in with the Waikiki Police and bring them up to speed. David, because he is still a police officer, will have the proper credentials and can present a letter from his commanding officer validating his status.

Gina and David will concentrate on Beaumont and bring her back. Our warrant is for anywhere in the US—and the State of Hawaii is part of the US. We won't have any extradition issues.

Next, Steve and Donny will locate and follow the Jamesons/ Peytons, confirming their location. Their warrants should be showing in the national crime database, so the local police should be able to arrest them.

Donny asked me if I could get a letter from DA Baxter authorizing them to *investigate* the Jamesons, which should also detail their charges and warrant information. I told him I'd get with Bill right after the meeting.

He's now looking across the table at us…asking our opinions. We're all smiling and saying it sounds like a solid plan…however, we know we have a few things left to do. Donny continues, saying it shouldn't take us more than four days, round trip. I told them I'd have Nelly start making the travel arrangements…did they want to leave tomorrow? Definitely, need to jump on this now…don't want to give them a chance to relocate! They looked at one another and said they'll get packed immediately.

I poked my head out of the conference room door. Nelly had finished with her families. I asked her to come back and bring a notepad. Anxious to hear what was going on, she ran back and grabbed a chair. Donny quickly brought her up to speed on the developments…asking her if she could make the travel arrangements for them if she had time. "You bet!" She rushed back and sat at Marla's desk, leaving her desk open in case a new client came in. She turned on Marla's computer and started inputting the necessary info.

While the team was talking with each other, going over the plan, I announced that Uncle Mike changed his schedule and will be arriving in a couple of days. But not to worry…I'll keep him busy until they return!

Donny sat with Nelly to help her with the travel plans. They found an early morning flight to Honolulu and a beautiful hotel a block from the beach…not that they were going to have time to play on the beach! But might as well get some rooms with a nice view! Donny reminded Nelly we will need four tickets going over, but *five tickets for the return flight!* The extra ticket for Beaumont!

It was going on 5:00 p.m. Marla would be in soon. Wait 'till she hears what's going on!

Before I head home, I wanted to call DA Baxter. I promised him I'd let him know what we decided. After three rings, Susie answered the phone and immediately connected me to Bill. After some minor teasing, something about me doing his job, I told him our plan… and the team was leaving in the morning. We're hopeful we can have this wrapped up in three days! I asked him if he could provide a letter authorizing the team to *investigate* the Jamesons…to eliminate any potential issues that may arise. He said he'd have Susie type it up before she goes home. I also asked him if he could contact the DA in Waikiki and the chief of police…to bring them into the loop. David will check in with them when they arrive…tomorrow afternoon.

Also, how did he want to handle the Jamesons? I told him *we* are planning on bringing Beaumont back. However, the Waikiki Police will have to arrest the Jamesons and make the arrangements for their return to the mainland. Bill said he'd call them now and help get our plan moving forward and call me back. He also mentioned he'd have Susie drop the letter off on her way home. Great! I'll be waiting for his call and a chance to see Susie!

Oh my gosh! After hanging up from Bill I remembered I forgot to discuss a very important issue with him! I quickly made a note to myself, so I wouldn't forget again. Thankfully, Bill called back within ten minutes. He told me the DA and the police chief are totally on board…anything we need, just let them know. They'll be so happy to get these people off their beautiful island!

Now, looking at my note, I asked him what would be the chances of seizing their assets…in the next couple of days. We don't want to do it now…it might interfere with our plan. I provided him with the condo addresses of Beaumont and the Jamesons…along with the information on their boats…not forgetting the property Jameson owned in San Francisco! He said, once he hears from me about their arrests, he'll get right on it! Hopefully, that will help in returning some of the monies they stole from their victims! I thanked him for everything and told him I'd call him tomorrow.

As I'm hanging up from Bill, Susie walks into the office with an envelope in her hand. She sees Nelly at Marla's computer and gives her a wink and a big hug. Donny, wanting some of this action, stands up and gives her his famous bear hug! We're all laughing as Susie walks back to my desk, takes a seat, and hands me the envelope. As I'm taking the letter from her, she clasps my hands and tells me how proud she and Bill are…how much we are helping them…and the county! They knew we'd do it! Wow! That was so wonderful to hear…we don't get many compliments!

* * *

Donny takes the envelope from my desk and places it in his briefcase. The travel arrangements are completed…plane, hotel, and car rental. The flight leaves at 6:20 a.m. and arrives in Honolulu at noon. Two rental cars have been reserved and four rooms at a beautiful hotel. Nelly prints out copies of the travel docs, one for each of them. The team will have to get to the airport by 4:00 a.m.! Glad it's them!

I update Donny on DA Baxter's phone call…about the police chief and DA in Waikiki…and about seizing the assets of Beaumont and the Jamesons.

Marla gets in and sees Nelly and Donny at her desk. She knows something is up. She heads back to my desk…looking curious and excited! I fill her in on the latest…now, she's really excited!

Donny calls the team and lets them know they need to be at the airport at 4:00 a.m. and he has all the travel documents.

I'm finally getting ready to head home. I see Nelly filling Marla in on the day's events. They seem to be doing some whispering…or maybe just talking softly!

Nelly turns her chair around to face me. Since the team is heading out for four days, and Uncle Mike is arriving in two days, she'll go back to her original *party plan* so the team can be here!

Darren lets Donny know he'll continue to run skip tracing on Beaumont and the Jamesons to monitor any new activities…credit card purchases, etc.

Time to call it a day. With so much happening, I know I won't be able to get much sleep…but will certainly try!

I get to the office at 6:30 a.m., my usual time. The team's on their way to Honolulu…and should arrive by noon. At about 5:00 a.m., I received a text from Gina telling me she'll get a beautiful picture of Hawaii for our photo wall! LOL!

Marla has several files on her desk…she posted three bonds during the night, for a total of $75,000 in bail! She's *definitely* a machine. The new clients should be in by noon to complete their portion of our paperwork.

She and I are trying to contain ourselves…we know these next couple of days are going to be fun and exciting! Especially since Uncle Mike gets in tomorrow!

I put on a fresh pot of coffee and grab a couple of files from her…wanting to help her put the new clients' info into our computer. Besides, I needed some busy work!

The morning passes by quite uneventfully…business as usual. Nelly got in at 7:30 a.m. One of our new clients came in a few minutes ago and completed his paperwork…two clients left. The phones have been ringing like crazy…we're able to schedule five more appointments for the day…busy…busy…busy! Is there a full moon?

I keep checking my watch…the team should be touching down soon in Honolulu. I made myself a note to text Gina to call me once they got situated.

Nelly has already printed out the info on our potential clients from the jail website…helping us to confirm the charges and bail amounts. I think she mentioned the combined bail amounts were $190,000! That would be nice…10 percent goes into our *kitty*.

Our first appointment arrived at nine thirty…with Darren coming in right behind them. After giving a hearty and cheerful "Good morning" to everyone, he headed directly to the investigator's office to start working.

Needing a cup of coffee, I got up and poured two cups…one for me, one for Darren.

Nelly is taking good care of our *new* clients, so I head back to the investigator's office. Darren's sitting at his desk with his briefcase open. He looks up and smiles…especially since I brought him coffee! He motions to me to grab a chair…he wanted to talk.

He said he was checking the Internet last night…just browsing…doing his usual skip tracing on our *bad boy/girl* cases…when a thought hit him! If the Jamesons are conducting business…their new scam…under the guise of "R and J Financial," maybe Beaumont is doing something similar! I love how my guys think…considering all the possibilities!

As I'm agreeing with him, he shows me a printout from a website. He explains how he mixed up the names, switching around the initials of the names, and finally, he hit *pay dirt*!

The printout, showing some beautiful homes, displayed the name "B and C Financial." The page listed the *partners* as *Christine* Beaumont and *Blake* Campbell! They had switched their last names… not too creative! And…OMG…in the center of the page were lovely pictures of "Christine" and "Blake" in an effort, I'm sure, to build trust and confidence in future clients! At the bottom of the page was listed a local phone number to call to schedule an appointment!

Now, Darren pointed to the very bottom of the page. In small print, it read "A Division of 'R and J Financial'"! He did it…Darren did it! Unbelievable! These people *really need* to go to jail…for a very long time! Who knows how many people, families, they have bilked! Stolen their life savings!

According to this web page, "B and C Financial" will help them acquire money from their homes and assist them in investing in their neighbors. So, that's their new scam! *Wow*! I asked Darren to text Donny and have him call us when he lands. We may need to rethink our *plan* on Beaumont. I also asked him to email the web page to Donny so he could have it when he arrived. I need to call Bill immediately.

This new info may save us a lot of time. The return plane tickets are for three days out…so they may actually have a little time to see some sights!

Nelly is still working with clients in the front office, so I called Bill from Darren's desk…didn't want our new clients overhearing my conversation.

Susie, naturally, answered the call. She said Bill's in court and should be back soon…she'll have him call me as soon as he returns.

As Nelly is finishing up with her first appointment, the second appointment arrives. Nelly directs them to the sofa, offers them coffee, and explains she'll be with them shortly.

I got up and grabbed the new client files from Nelly and started filling out the bail bond. I call the jail to make sure I have the necessary and correct info for the bail bond. Done and done!

It just dawned on me…Bill is in court for the sentencing hearings on Montgomery, Peyton, Vasquez, Caravello, and Campbell! Can't wait to hear from him!

Hearing Nelly describe the bail process to our second appointment/client, I smile with great pride! They decided to proceed in bailing out their father. Apparently, the father got in a bar fight, causing a fellow patron to be taken to the hospital! Oops!

When she finished with this new client, I prepped the bail bond. I told her I'd walk both bonds to the jail. It'll give me a break and a chance to see some of my deputy buddies. I need a diversion!

* * *

As I'm walking out the door, headed to the jail, our third scheduled appointment arrives. I tell Nelly I'm going to stop at Bill's office on my way back. She nods her head and starts working with our new potential client.

With the two bonds in hand, I remembered I wanted to take Bill a copy of Beaumont's web page. After retrieving a copy from Darren, I *now* head out! Places to go…people to see!

It's 11:45 a.m. The team should be arriving shortly. Bill should be back in his office…the court takes a lunch recess at twelve.

After dropping off the bail bonds and schmoozing with my buddies, I make my way to his office…really anxious and excited to tell him our new info.

Walking through the door, I see Susie munching on a salad. She's nodding her head and pointing to Bill's office. Setting down her fork, she tells me he just got in. It's lunchtime…OMG…I'll pick up food on my way back to the office.

As I enter Bill's office, he's putting down his phone…saying he was just going to call me. He gave me a rundown on the morning events. Lisa Montgomery and Samuel Peyton received "time served with three years' probation" as he talked about earlier. However, the judge was quite angry. Christine Campbell, Sarah Vasquez, and Dean Caravello were at the center of the judge's anger. He detailed the pain they inflicted on hundreds of trusting people…stealing their life savings. He did not accept the proposed fifteen-year sentence… he imposed a "twenty-year sentence, with no parole and a restitution bill of over \$4,000,000!"

Bill, with a slight grin on his face, continued saying he thinks this will be the same judge presiding over Beaumont and the Jamesons… and thinks he will impose the same sentence on them!

It's been a great day, so far! Susie brings us each a cup of coffee and hands Bill an apple. She winks at me and then returns to her desk. Bill shrugs his shoulders…knowing he can't argue with her!

He could see I was excited about something! I reached inside my jacket and pulled out the copy of Beaumont's website…telling him this has been burning a hole in my pocket for the last hour!

As he is reading it, I can see the anger building in his expression! I give him a recap of what the team is doing…they arrived about an hour ago. But I tell Bill, this new info may help us locate her faster…and maybe even the Jamesons!

He grabs his apple and starts tossing it in the air…playing catch with it. I can see the anger somewhat subsiding now. Knowing him as I do, I see a *plan* is developing in his brain! Setting the apple back on his desk, he tells me he needs to call Judge Miller immediately! This is my hint to leave…he's coming up with something! I told him, as always, I'll keep him posted on the team's status.

I finally get a text from Gina…they landed and are on their way to pick up the rental cars. As I finished reading her text, my cell phone rang…it's Donny. He saw the Beaumont web page Darren emailed him. I told him to get situated in their rooms at the hotel, then call me back…telling him I'd have Darren standing by.

We still have clients in the office, so I decided to make myself comfortable at Gina's desk. I told Darren about Bill's reaction to the Beaumont web page and about the judge at the hearing. He imposed a twenty-year sentence on all of them, except Montgomery and Peyton. Even hitting them with a restitution bill!

I mentioned Bill thinks the judge will also impose the same sentence on Beaumont and the Jamesons. Also…I think he's up to something…and planning on meeting with Judge Miller right away! Go get 'em, Bill!

As I was at the jail and Bill's office, Darren said he'd been doing some more digging. He was able to search the property records for the State of Hawaii…and found twenty-three new *refis* during the last seven months. And, digging still deeper, mainly into the business activities of "B and C Financial" and "R and J Financial," he discovered nine of these *refis* invested their money with either "B and C" or "R and J" Financial. And as near as he could figure, they have *stolen* over \$3,000,000! OMG!

I called Bill immediately. Susie said he just left to meet with Judge Miller. I gave her this new info and asked her to get it to Bill ASAP…he might need it when he talks to Judge Miller. Right away!

My brain has been in overdrive all morning…I forgot to pick up food for us. I called our corner burger joint and asked if they could deliver some burgers, fries, and drinks. No problem…give them twenty minutes.

Darren and I are still discussing this new info…and what totally despicable people they are! As we're waiting for Donny to call, our lunch order arrives and he hands the box of food to Nelly.

Having finished up with client #3, she can join us in the investigator's office for a quick bite. She sets the buzzer on the front door, so we can hear if anyone enters…and brings the food back. Since she's been so busy with clients all morning, Darren and I start telling her the new info…showing her the printout from Beaumont's web page. Darren mentioned the $3,000,000 they may have already stolen from *trusting investors*!

I tell her we're waiting on a call from Donny…we may have to change our plan a little! Also, I'm sure Bill will call us this afternoon…after his meeting with Judge Miller.

* * *

Donny finally calls…they're all in his room and his phone is on *speaker*. David starts off with the traditional "Aloha" greeting…saying how beautiful the hotel is…a block from the beach…and hopes they can enjoy a little of the sun and beach! Maybe even some surfing! We'll see…maybe! Gina is saying she'd love to work on her tan!

Donny jumps in…trying to contain his crazy team! He says they have studied the printout on Beaumont. They discussed an alternate plan: call and get an appointment with Beaumont and arrest her when she shows! Even though they were looking forward to seeing her fifty-five-foot houseboat!

Gina added she thinks she can convince Beaumont to bring the Jamesons to the appointment…using her feminine wiles! The guys agreed to proceed in that direction. I then relayed the earlier conversation I had with Bill…again, highlighting his anger. Telling them, also, I think he is up to something and I'll let them know as soon as possible.

Before hanging up, Darren mentioned the $3 million they may have stolen already from the people of Hawaii…and it only took them six months!

Gina said she'll start calling the number listed on the web page and try to get an appointment for tomorrow morning. She'll stress the fact she is with three other friends that might also be interested in *investing* with them. This tactic may force her to invite the Jamesons…to help seal the deal!

I agreed and told them to keep us posted…and to save their receipts!

Now, it's a waiting game…waiting to hear back from Gina and waiting to hear from Bill. Patience!

I must appear to be *virtuous* today…Bill's call came in. Still in the investigator's office, I put his call on speaker so Nelly, Darren, and I could all hear. Bill explains he showed all the docs…the print-outs…to Judge Miller. He saw these pages detailed their continuing scams…also the $3 million they have already bilked out of the people of Hawaii.

Needing no further convincing, Judge Miller immediately ordered "no bail" warrants on Blake Beaumont, Rudolph Jameson, and Judith Jameson! Once we get them arrested, they will stay in custody until they appear before *him* in court!

Bill also asked if we would be willing to bring back the Jamesons along with Beaumont. He can get the necessary paperwork to us… and knowing we'd be willing, he already informed the DA and chief of police. They are fully on board!

The "no bail" warrants should be showing in the criminal database system now. *Judge Miller really wants these people and wants them now!*

I told Bill we may have them tomorrow…giving him our latest update. And, oh, Bill said he forgot one last important thing. The county will be picking up the tab for this investigation. The judge said it was the least they could do…considering the great job we've done!

Wow! Wow! Wow!

Trying to recover from our shock, Darren, Nelly and I look at one another with big smiles! It's great to be appreciated and actually recognized for our hard work! We all thanked Bill…expressing our deep gratitude!

I told him we'd call him when we get set up for the appointment tomorrow. I also reminded him we would probably need the Waikiki Police at the meeting to arrest the Jamesons…*not in the meeting*… just at the location, undercover! He said to let him know the time and place for the meeting and he'd call the chief of police…they're ready!

Within minutes, Donny calls. We're all on speaker. He proceeds to tell me, Gina, in her sweet Southern accent, got a hold of Blake/Christine Beaumont and set an appointment for 10 a.m. tomorrow morning…at their office. They have an office! He gives me the address. Gina jumps into the conversation. We hear David and Steve in the background…teasing her. She says she wanted to appear to be a little naïve and gullible when she spoke to Beaumont…she needed to have the *sound of money* dripping from her mouth! And it worked! After first talking with Beaumont's secretary, she was immediately connected to Beaumont herself. She took the bait…hook, line, and sinker!

Then, Gina said, appearing absentminded, she tells her she forgot she has three other friends who are also interested in investing. Beaumont asked her to please invite them along. She has some associates that would love to join them and answer any questions they may have. Could this be the Jamesons?

We're all laughing, not only along with Gina but also about the fun time they'll be having tomorrow! We told them all *great job*. And I'll get this info to Bill ASAP!

I also mentioned that David may want to contact the chief of police…mainly to introduce himself and make sure we're all on the same page. No problem…he'll call him right now.

Before hanging up, I told them the county is picking up our tab…so make sure you save your receipts! David hollers out, "I know a great sushi restaurant!" I tell them to have fun and be safe. They have the night free…but need to be ready for tomorrow.

I waited a few minutes, then called Bill. I gave him the time and location for tomorrow's meeting…adding I think the Jamesons will also be present. I told him David is checking in with the chief of police now to coordinate everything. Perfect!

* * *

It's been a great…and busy…day! Nelly completed the paperwork on four out of five clients so far. The last client is scheduled to come in at 6:00 p.m. If all goes well, we will have posted eight bonds for the day, totaling $265,000 in bail…a really great day! And we should have our $150,000 fugitive in custody tomorrow…along with her sidekicks!

Marla arrived at the office an hour early. She knew there would be a lot going on…and wanted to be a part of it. Besides, she wanted to help Nelly with the plans for Uncle Mike's party.

She looks out over the office. Darren is still here and I'm still here…she was right…there's been a lot happening! Oh-oh! No coffee! So, before settling in, she puts on two fresh pots of coffee and makes sure her boom box is playing her good old rock and roll!

Nelly's entering new client info into the computer…and she's ready for the six o'clock appointment. Marla sits down with her and gets the recap of the day's events: (1) the bonds posted; (2) the clients needing to come in to complete their paperwork; (3) the six o'clock appointment; (4) new files needing to be input into computer; and (5) the team's adventure in Waikiki, so far.

Marla *high-fives* Nelly and starts doing her *happy dance* all the way back to my desk. I'm shaking my head, laughing at her. She's singing the song "Tomorrow" as she heads my way! All of a sudden, I hear a deep voice coming from the investigator's office…Darren is joining in on Marla's song: "Tomorrow, tomorrow, you're only a day away!" Then, Nelly joins in…and what the heck…I join in! We've even joined Marla in her crazy *happy dance* routine! Thank goodness, there are no clients in the office! Thanks, Marla…we needed this break from reality…everyone's been working so hard.

Trying to settle back down and regain our composure, Nelly reminds me Uncle Mike will be arriving tomorrow at about 2:00 p.m.! OMG…that's right…these days have just flown by! She tells me the party plans are coming along just fine…everything is on schedule! On schedule? What is she doing?

Saved by the bell! Or should I say cell phone? It was David… on speaker. Darren and I step back into the investigator's office and place my cell phone on speaker as well. David tells us he just spoke to Police Chief Higgins. He'll have four of his officers arrive at 7:00 a.m. to get positioned around the office building. We figured the staff would probably get in at eight…so he wanted his officers in place prior. Sergeant Jones will be heading up his team. If the Jamesons do show, his officers will take them all into custody…and hold them for us!

David continued saying if all goes as planned tomorrow, Donny, Steve, Gina and I decided to return a day early…coming back the day after tomorrow. Steve has already checked airline availability and there are seats available…and Chief Higgins has made arrangements for two US marshals to accompany us on the return trip…just to be on the safe side!

We told David how impressed we were with the extent of their operation. David said to *thank* Bill Baxter. Bill made sure everything, and everyone, was available to assist…in whatever we needed!

Steve said he's not making the airline reservations yet…he wants to make sure we have the Jamesons first! Sounds good to me. I can hear Donny and Gina in the background…something about a sunset dinner cruise! Gina yells out, "I'm getting lots of pictures!"

Darren and I tell them to have a great time, enjoy…and call us in the morning. My *Hawaii team* signed off with their "Aloha" saying the island magic is calling to them. I could picture Gina doing her hula dance!

I head back up to the front…Darren is packing it in for the day. He'll be back at eight in the morning. Nelly's getting ready to take off, also. She's sitting at Marla's desk…going over files…so it seemed! I told them about David's call…if all goes as planned tomorrow, they'll be coming back a day early…hopefully, with two additional *guests*! Nelly looked a little concerned…but I told her Steve will make all the return flight arrangements. She seemed relieved!

Marla's ready for whatever the night brings her. She's all set up and waiting for the last appointment. Her coffee is on…the music is playing…she's definitely set for the evening!

Nelly finally leaves to get home to her kids. Darren and I walk out…anticipating the upcoming events. We love it when a plan comes together!

* * *

The big day arrives. I'm in the office at 6:30 a.m. Marla looks so energized…or should I say *caffeinated*! She looks at me in disappointment…"What, no donuts?" Okay…okay…I can take a hint. As she puts on a fresh pot of coffee, I walk next door to Dee Dee's and get two dozen donuts. I laugh and tell her Marla is going through withdrawals! As she's boxing up the donuts, I tell her Uncle Mike is coming in this afternoon and would love to see her. I see her smiling at the mention of Uncle Mike…and says it'll be great to see him again!

All boxed up, I get back to the office. The coffee is done, the donuts are here…all is good with the world! We each pour a cup of coffee and grab a donut. I sit with her at her desk. She gives me a rundown of the night's activities. Our 6:00 p.m. appointment made it in…paperwork completed. She even had time to run the bail bond over to the jail. This new client should be in this morning to finish his portion of the paperwork. She continued by saying two new clients *walked in* about midnight to bail out their friends. Surprisingly, their credit check came back as acceptable, was solid in the community, and paid the premium in cash. She has the bonds ready to post with the jail but is planning on dropping them off on her way home. These two bonds were for minor drug offenses…the bail for each was $10,000…so $20,000 altogether.

She did a great job. She added we only have one scheduled appointment for today…so far!

We both finished our *first* donut and cup of coffee. I told her to get moving…she needed to deliver the bonds…and get home. Still, kind of in her *happy dance* mood, she told me she'd be back early… she didn't want to miss out on any of the action! I hugged her good-bye…and sent her on her way.

I'm a note person. I *have* to write things down, or I'll forget them. My first note: wait for a call from the team; next, Uncle Mike arrives this afternoon; next, keep Bill Baxter apprised of the events. That's all I can think of for the time being.

It's, again, a waiting game! I'm not a *wait-er*…but I've learned patience over the years!

Nelly gets in…right on time…and notices the anxiety on my face. My *laugh line*s are betraying me! She brings me over another donut and refills my coffee. She looks at Marla's desk…then her desk…only a couple of files. Good, she thinks. She has things to take care of today…and needs the time.

I give her a brief rundown on the night's activities…somewhat busy…but quiet. We should have four new clients coming in today to complete their paperwork…and we have one scheduled appointment for later. I tell her I'm waiting for the team to call…and I know they will soon.

Finally, David called! He received a call from Sergeant Jones. His team is in place at the location. David told him they'd get there around nine forty five…just prior to the meeting. If the Jamesons show up, he'll step out of the meeting…pretending to take a phone call. Sounds great. He told me this is where I come in…he needs me to call his cell at about ten fifteen…giving him the excuse to take the call, in private outside. I can do that!

Once Sergeant Jones sees David, his team will advance and make the apprehensions! Works for me!

I knew David had me on speaker, I could hear Donny and Gina teasing each other in the background. I asked them if they had a nice time last night. They each chimed in…the cruise around the harbor was beautiful; the food was great and wonderful entertainment.

Donny spoke up…saying they were at breakfast now…getting *fortified* for the meeting. He said he'd call me after…to confirm their departure for tomorrow…with their additional *guests*. Steve will make the new flight arrangements.

I could still hear the playful bantering in the background! Gina is saying, "Tell her…tell her!" What? Donny starts laughing and tells me *he* is treating the team to an authentic luau tonight. They're all looking forward to it…should be lots of fun! I wished them luck. I was very happy they're squeezing in some fun while there.

As I was hanging up from Donny, Darren walked in…with something on his arm! Nelly rushed over to him and picks up a cute puppy! He introduces us to "Max." His German shepherd puppy. He's the new addition to his family. Grinning from ear to ear, Darren tells us he got Max from the kid we arrested a couple of weeks ago… the guy who was selling the German shepherd puppies. Oh yeah…I remember. He had been thinking about getting a dog…so he did! He's been training Max for a week…he's pretty smart…and *house-trained*!

Good for him…but I repeat…we do *not* need a mascot! I asked him to keep Max in the back office…didn't want him scaring our clients. Darren said he just brought him in to meet us…he'll take him back home in a few minutes. Nelly, still fussing over and playing with Max, gave him a hug goodbye…she now has a new man in her life, Max!

Checking my watch, I see it's nine…good! I shot Bill a quick text saying, "Running smoothly…everyone in place." Not long now. I hear Nelly on the phone…talking softly…saying something about Uncle Mike and how much fun it's going to be! Now I know she's up to something…and who was she talking to? She suspected I over-heard her conversation. She turns her chair around to face me and says Susie just called to wish us luck! Hmmm! I didn't hear the phone ring…hmmm!

The next few minutes seem to drag by…what's the saying, "A watched pot never boils"? At long last, I get a text from David…they just arrived for the meeting…going to wait a few minutes before they enter the building. And…please remember to call him at ten fifteen. Police in place.

I'm sitting on pins and needles…counting the minutes and watching the clock…ten fifteen can't get here soon enough! Appearing to be talking jokingly amongst themselves, they enter the "B and C Financial" office…with Gina in the lead. She introduces herself to the receptionist and says they have a ten o'clock appointment with Ms. Beaumont. The receptionist rings Beaumont, saying her ten o'clock appointment is here.

Beaumont saunters out of her office...dressed impeccably... looking like the ultimate successful businesswoman. Gina, still in her southern drawl, introduces herself and her three friends. Beaumont shows them to a large office. Gina proceeds by saying they are all here to vacation...probably stay two...maybe three...weeks...but it all depends on how things are going back home. They're from Alabama...and are sure enjoying the sun and warmth of the islands.

David starts adding they are seriously considering buying property in Waikiki...as a winter getaway...and would like to find a sound business opportunity to invest in as well.

Steve interjects...back home they all "dabble a little" in some oil fields...which were passed on to them from their parents...however, his real love in life is raising cattle!

They could see Beaumont *licking her chops*! Probably thinking she has some really easy *targets* sitting in front of her. She now mentions she has her fellow associates...really partners...in another office and would like to invite them to join in...so confident they'd have some great ideas. She left the office and returned quickly with her two fellow *associates/partners*. Sure enough, as they had hoped...it was the Jamesons! She introduced them as "Rudy and Judy Peyton."

Within seconds, ten fifteen sharp...David's cell phone rings. He excuses himself, saying he needs to take the call...and walks outside. That was the signal for Sergeant Jones and his team. They quickly rushed the office and barged into the meeting with weapons pointed and ordered everyone on the ground!

David, being so thoughtful, kept his cell phone on so I could hear everything...loud voices, mainly from the officers...and other voices *demanding* an explanation!

Sergeant Jones looked at David...giving him the honor of placing them all under arrest! David went to Blake Beaumont, then Rudolph Jameson, and lastly, Judith Jameson...calling them by their *real names*! A defeated look came over them...they knew they were caught...but couldn't figure out how!

While Sergeant Jones and his officers were busy *cuffing* the three fugitives, Donny let it slip that their friends, Campbell, Vasquez, and Caravello, were just sentenced to twenty years in state prison! Now they really looked scared and nervous! The police officers hauled them off…very happy to lock them up in Waikiki jail!

The team thanked Sergeant Jones and his team, telling them they'd stop by in a couple of hours to confirm the travel arrangements for tomorrow.

I'm still listening in…and jumping up and down in my chair! Nelly is doing the *happy dance* and Darren is singing "Bad Boys… Bad Boys!" David gets back on the line…I could hear the excitement in his voice. He tells me they'll call us later…in about an hour.

I had to call Bill immediately. Susie answered and put me right through. All I said…had to say…was "All in custody." The team, along with his two appointed US marshals, will be delivering them tomorrow. He was so happy. He said he can now get the "asset seizure" paperwork filed…Judge Miller signed off on it earlier.

A couple of days ago, I gave Bill a listing of the properties these *fine people* owned. The properties they stole from others! One home in the San Francisco area, two condos in Waikiki, and two boats. We were pretty sure there were more properties out there…but that's what we found so far. The value of these *stolen properties* totaled over $5 million! Moneys that can, hopefully, be returned to their victims.

Bill said he'd call Judge Miller. The judge wanted to know when these people would be in his courtroom! I laughed, along with Bill. He said he'd see me soon, then hung up.

CHAPTER 10

———

The Hammer of Justice

The team was exhilarated now! It was terrific to see the police placing them in the patrol cars…they won't be able to hurt any more people! Gina, true to her word, got a great picture of their faces as they were being marched out of their office…for the photo wall?

They decided to celebrate. They saw a restaurant/bar right on the beach…you can actually sit at a table on the beach, under an umbrella and enjoy the view. That's the one. David and Gina got there first, with Donny and Steve arriving seconds later. Steve was carrying his laptop…had the last bit of work to do.

What a beautiful view. You could reach out and touch the ocean…they were literally sitting six feet from the water's edge. Situated at their table and orders placed, Steve pulled out his laptop to make sure the flights were still available for tomorrow. *Need seven seats*! Yahoo!

After a few minutes, he found a flight leaving at 7:30 a.m… that'll work. He copied the flight info down and also sent it to his phone. They needed to get this info to Chief Higgins so he can have the three fugitives ready for transport…and pass the info onto the marshals.

But for the next hour, they're going to relax and enjoy themselves. Besides, it'll take Sergeant Jones an hour or so to book them in…mug shots, prints, the whole ball of wax!

Sitting outside, enjoying the sun and the island breeze, they thought they had better call me…especially since they have the flight information.

According to the clock on the wall, it's 11:05 a.m. It's been a great morning. My cell phone rings…it's Donny on speaker. Before Donny can say anything, Gina thanks me…they are having a wonderful time…especially now that their job is over! She's going on about *everything Hawaiian* when Donny takes over…laughing at her. Okay…Okay…I think DJ gets the picture!

He tells me Steve got the flight lined up…leaves at 7:30 a.m., so they'll have to get to the airport by 5:00 a.m…picking up their extra passengers along the way! The flight arrives home at 1:15 p.m. They'll go directly from the airport to the jail…and *gladly* deliver their fugitives! They should be at the jail no later than 2:00 p.m.

David jumps into the conversation saying they'll drop off the flight schedule to Chief Higgins and Sergeant Jones…letting them know they'll pick up their prisoners at 4:30 a.m.

As he's talking, I can actually hear the waves breaking in the background…and the Hawaiian music playing softly. I'm so jealous!

Donny reminded me they're going to the luau tonight…did I want them to bring me anything back? How about a pineapple and a lei?

I'm so happy they have time to relax and enjoy the island. I signed off by telling them to have a wonderful time…keep Gina under control, and text…or call…me before they board the plane in the morning. It's a deal!

Now it's time for *me* to relax. Nelly and I are savoring our coffee…saying we wish we could have seen Beaumont's face! David mentioned Beaumont asked how we found her! He told her, "We just followed your crumbs…you're not as special as you think you are!"

We were laughing. I decided I wanted to be in the courtroom when they appear before Judge Miller…I want to see their faces in person!

The office was quiet…no clients. So I called Bill and gave him the flight info…saying they should get to the jail around 2:00

p.m. He was very pleased and said he'd get them added on to Judge Miller's calendar for the following morning! Plus, he'd let Judge Miller know to expect them! He also mentioned he contacted some of their victims…people they stole from. They will be in the courtroom also. What a great idea…let them face the people they *conned and scammed*! I'm definitely going to be in the courtroom now… gotta see this!

The rest of the morning flies by…business as usual…now that our adventure is completed. Uncle Mike should be arriving soon…I expect he'll stop by the office around three thirty…after he gets checked in at the hotel.

Nelly picked up some crepe streamers on her way home last night…part of her *party plan*? We start hanging them all over the office. She even made a "Welcome Home, Mike" sign…three by five feet…which she wants to hang in the front window. No argument from me…I like the plan so far! He'll love it.

I don't expect Darren in today…he deserves some time off… besides, he needs to spend time with Max.

Nelly and I are staying busy…cleaning the office! Dusting the desks, chairs, tables, computers…everything. We want the office to *sparkle* when Uncle Mike walks in.

Standing back to admire our work, we concurred the streamers look great, the sign looks great, and the office, indeed, sparkles! All we now need is Uncle Mike!

He sent me a text twenty minutes ago saying they landed and are on their way to the hotel. He expects they'll be at the office by four. They! They? What's he saying? Aside from my curiosity over the *mysterious envelope* I *now really wonder* what he's up to! Only have to wait another hour or so!

CHAPTER 11

Uncle Mike Cometh!

All of a sudden, I hear horns honking, voices yelling, "Hey…hi… great to see ya…welcome back!" I look up and out the front window. A group of people are huddled around a couple…laughing, shaking hands, slapping each other on the back, and hugging one another!

I recognized some of the people in the group…a few of my deputy buddies and office neighbors…including Dee Dee!

My curiosity takes over. I walked out to see what all the commotion was about. At the center of the group is *Uncle Mike*…surrounded by his friends! Making my way through the crowd, getting hugs along the way, I rush to Uncle Mike and give him *my biggest bear hug*!

His friends, our friends, are starting to return to their work and offices. As the crowd is thinning out, I see two bags of Florida oranges sitting on the ground next to Uncle Mike…and an attractive lady standing next to him!

He sees I have noticed this lady. He takes my hand…and hers… and introduces her: Diane Faraday. How exciting for Uncle Mike! Soooo…I do the only thing I can do…give her a huge hug also.

He picks up the bags of oranges. I take Diane's hand, and we all walk to the office. As we enter, Nelly sees Uncle Mike and runs to greet him…also noticing Diane. He sees all the decorations in the office, especially the sign in the window, and starts tearing up a bit.

Diane, seeing the emotion, gives Nelly a hug and declares she has never seen a *welcome party* such as this!

Now catching his breath, and composure, he takes Diane's hand and formally introduces her. This is Diane…Diane Faraday. She's a retired criminal court judge…retired for the last eight years. And… we've been *keeping company* for about the last two years.

Nelly and I are smiling big-time now! Good for both of them. He continued saying they have a lot in common…him, a law enforcement background, and her, a retired judge. How perfect! Diane, slightly laughing, says between the two of them, they are *always* the main entertainment at parties…each telling stories about their jobs…the many crazy situations they got involved in!

I showed Diane around the office and told them both about our Waikiki adventure…detailing everything! I told her she would meet the rest of the team tomorrow night…we're all going to dinner. She was excited to meet everyone…and very happy to *finally* meet me!

While we're all still laughing and talking, Marla gets in and runs to Uncle Mike. They seem to be whispering to one another… even turning to Nelly…keeping their comments between the three of them. Diane, in an attempt to distract me, says they would like to invite me to join them for dinner tonight…just the three of us… so we can catch up on things! I'll say! Okay…six thirty it is…they'll pick me up at the office.

They turn to leave. I call after them, "No you don't…not so fast! What about *my envelope*?" He says they need to get to Bill's office. He wants Diane to meet him. "What about my envelope?" Uncle Mike takes Diane's hand as they're walking out the door and says, "You have to wait until tomorrow night!" They're testing my virtue! My patience! I know I can't win. So, I tell them I'd see them at six thirty for dinner.

After leaving I see them head toward Bill's office. It's been a couple of years since they've seen one another…plus Bill will love meeting Diane! Nelly, Marla, and I, each smiling, say how great it is to see

Uncle Mike…and especially meet Diane. She seems wonderful…I'm looking forward to dinner tonight…to get to know her a little better!

* * *

Right on time…six thirty. Uncle Mike pulls up in front of the office. Before he can get out, I run to the car. Diane is in the front passenger seat…I jump in the back. Both Nelly and Marla come out and wave goodbye…telling us to have a great time!

He made reservations at the local steak house…perfect choice! I haven't had a steak in ages. We're shown to a table by the window… he wanted Diane to take in all the beauty of our little town. The glimmering lights from the storefronts and the friendly people passing by.

We ordered our drinks and got comfortable. He asked me to tell her about some of our crazy adventures…some of our recent escapades…I'd love to!

Diane, having been a lawyer for many years and a judge for over fifteen years, knew how the bail process worked. But she didn't realize what we went through to apprehend our clients that jump bail.

I started my monologue with the adventure we had in Las Vegas, about eight months ago. Giving her a brief synopsis of the events… and how we found him through various social media platforms. His girlfriend had posted that they were getting married on such and such day, even listing the address of the wedding chapel in Vegas. Needless to say, he didn't make it to the altar!

They were both shaking their heads…giggling about the stupidity of some people. I really like Diane…and I see the way she looks at Uncle Mike!

Still being the proud uncle, he asks me to tell her about our Paris adventure…saying it was *one for the books*! As I'm taking a sip of my wine, getting ready to start on another story, I see Bill walk into the restaurant and toward our table. Uncle Mike motions to me to slide over in the booth to make room for Bill. Gladly! Diane pops up, saying they invited him to join us…besides, he has some news for you! First, Bill orders a glass of beer and gets comfortable.

Well…what's the news? He said he spoke to the DA in Waikiki earlier…just to give him an update…our three criminals will be in court tomorrow. The DA mentioned they have started an investigation into their business activities in Waikiki. They have found quite a few *victims* and will be filing charges against them within the next couple of days! So, they might be extradited back to Hawaii once they are sentenced here!

The news made us all very happy. Bill also mentioned the Waikiki DA and police chief want to use them as an example to hopefully deter other criminals from scamming their citizens!

We all raised our glasses and toasted on that news! The waiter returned, bringing another round of drinks…and we placed our dinner order. While waiting for our dinner, Uncle Mike urges me to tell Diane about our Paris adventure. Bill, laughs, saying this is a good one…he even got involved!

Okay…okay…you win!

It was a $500,000 skip…a $1 million warrant! Very wealthy family…owned several wineries, here and in Paris. The man had kidnapped his daughter. We, the team and I, tracked him all over California, from his winery here to a casino he frequented, to the university he taught at…and finally, to Paris!

Long story short, the team confirmed his location in Paris and developed a very creative *ruse* to get him to return to California… which he did! We even sent a team to Paris, to follow him and make sure he boarded the plane for his return. Gina and Darren had a wonderful time in Paris…the City of Lights!

Once the plane landed in Northern California, and he stepped off the plane, Donny and David arrested him and brought him back. I went on to explain there were a lot of twists and turns with the case…too many to mention now. Besides, I see the waiter bringing our dinner!

After thoroughly enjoying our dinner, our drinks, and the playful banter, we bid each other good night and said we'd see Bill in the morning…in the courtroom! We all wanted to attend the hearing… should be interesting and fun.

Uncle Mike and Diane headed back to their hotel. Bill dropped me off at the office. Marla was holding the office down…no clients, but we had a couple appointments scheduled…and she's ready for them. I hear the music playing…see two pots of coffee on…she's definitely ready!

I pat her shoulder and tell her I'll see her in the morning…we have an interesting day ahead of us!

CHAPTER 12

Time to Face the Music!

The day has finally arrived…the day Beaumont and the Jamesons face their victims, Bill and Judge Miller! It's going to be a lovely day! Can you hear the sarcasm in my voice?

It's 6:30 a.m., my usual time to arrive at the office. Marla is her perky self…however, I did notice a little extra energy in her movements! This time I don't think it's the caffeine!

She's walking around the office…really *dancing* around the office…having fun! Before I make it back to my desk, she catches me and twirls me around! Laughing, I ask her if she's alright. Standing by the coffeepot now and adjusting the music on her boom box, she looks at me with a devilish grin and says, "We have the hearing this morning…and those snakes are going to feel the hand of the justice system! Yes…it's going to be a great day!" "And we have Uncle Mike's party tonight!" Also saying she is going to the hearing with us.

Now I understand and fully agree with her. I had to admit I was just as excited as she was about the upcoming events of the day!

The court starts at nine, and the doors to the courtroom open at eight thirty…so we need to get there by eight fifteen. The entire team is going to be there…they wouldn't miss it!

The team arrived yesterday from Honolulu, with the three fugitives in tow. The Waikiki Police had the prisoners ready for transport at 4:30 a.m., as planned. The two US marshals, Wilkes and Booth (no kidding), were present and took possession of the prisoners.

Everything went smoothly at the airport, and the flight was uneventful. Donny and Gina noticed some of the other passengers staring at our prisoners from time to time…but quickly turned away when we caught them. People are just curious…that's all!

They were booked into the local jail by 2:30 p.m…and were told their attorneys were on the way.

DA Baxter…Bill…made sure some of his assistants were available to meet with the *now inmates* and their attorneys. He wanted to see if they could agree upon a *sentence*. He didn't want to take these cases to trial…Besides, the evidence was overwhelming.

Marla put on two pots of fresh coffee. She knows *everyone* was meeting at the office before walking over to the courthouse. So thoughtful!

Donny and David were the first to arrive…they even had a little extra bounce in their step. Darren and Steve show up a few minutes later…and everyone is grabbing a cup of Marla's famous coffee! Boy, does she know the team!

It's about seven thirty now, and we're all talking about the events of the last couple of days: the beauty of the island, beaches, the weather, food, the luau…and, oh, the arrest of the criminals!

We all love our adventures. We never know where our cases will take us…but we're ready to go wherever we need to!

Gina finally arrives…carrying a small package, wrapped in *balloon paper*. I look at her and the team…wondering what's up. They form a circle around my desk as Gina hands me the package. I start tearing off the wrapping paper…curious about its contents. I see two silver-plated frames. In the first frame was a beautiful picture of Waikiki Beach, highlighting the coast and Diamond Head. The second frame displayed a picture of Donny, Steve, David, and Gina having drinks on the beach…definitely enjoying themselves. "So…so… cute! Thank you very much! However, did you forget something?" They all look at one another confused…what was I talking about? "I remember *something* about *somebody* bringing me a pineapple and lei!" LOL!

Marla and Nelly are admiring the beauty of the island…and commenting about the drinks on the beach! Gina then exclaims, "Pictures for the photo wall!" Perfect…they will make a wonderful addition! She hands me some more pictures…pictures of Beaumont and the Jamesons being arrested! It wasn't their best side…don't think they will want to add it to their website! We can't put these pictures on the wall, but we can certainly enjoy looking at them. Nelly and Marla are making their comments…something about scum, thieves, and crooks!

Uncle Mike and Diane walk through the door. They see the whole team assembled…and the colorful decorations still hanging up in the office. We have a few minutes before we have to leave for the courthouse…so I show them the pictures of Waikiki…especially those of Beaumont and the Jamesons! You could see the pride on Uncle Mike's face…he taught me well! Diane, now having a better idea of what we go through to apprehend the criminals, congratulates the team…well done! She even made a couple of *colorful* comments about Beaumont and the Jamesons. I knew I was going to like this lady!

Time to make our way to the courthouse…a short walk…a good stretch of the legs!

* * *

Right on schedule…the courtroom doors opened at eight thirty. We entered…knowing we'd need an entire bench to accommodate all of us: Donny, David, Gina, Darren, Steve, Uncle Mike, Diane, Marla, and me!

Other people are filing into the courtroom…probably there to support their family or friends that had cases on the calendar this morning.

I see Bill and three of his assistants enter the courtroom and take their seats at the prosecution table. Each was carrying multiple case files…some rather large!

Judge Miller enters through the back door and approaches his *bench.* The bailiff asks all in the audience to please rise. He announces court is now in session. "Judge Anthony Miller presiding. Please be seated."

Judge Miller takes the bench and starts reviewing the case files. He calls the first case and handles it expeditiously. He calls six more cases and resolves them…some with fines, a few were given future court dates, and some accepted jail time in lieu of paying fines.

As he is dispensing with these cases, people are leaving the courtroom…the cases for their friends and family had been settled. Judge Miller now calls for a ten-minute recess…and whispers something to his bailiff. Bill turns around, looks at us, and nods his head. We know what's coming!

We hear a metal latch click and see the steel mesh door open on the opposite side of the courtroom.

The bailiff is directing Blake Beaumont, Rudolph Jameson, and Judith Jameson into the metal *cage*. They are shackled together and have to take baby steps to position themselves. Perfect…so befitting! The humiliation is showing on Beaumont's face! Great! We see their attorneys step toward the *cage* and start conferring with their clients.

Judge Miller returns to the bench. There are probably twenty people left in the courtroom at this point. He pulls out three hefty case files from his stack…and calls the cases on Beaumont and the Jamesons. Their attorneys have them rise and face the judge. They introduce themselves, as attorneys for the defendants, and for the record. Bill stands and identifies himself for the record: "DA Baxter for the prosecution."

Judge Miller is reviewing the three case files…definitely not happy. Bill begins to enumerate the many charges of fraud, ID theft, property theft…plus the multitude of other charges against these defendants. He details their *scam process*, the number of homes/properties they have stolen…he even mentions how they continued their *scam* in the State of Hawaii. Bill continues to detail the millions of dollars their fraudulent schemes netted them!

Catching his breath, he looks around the courtroom and sees the five families he asked to appear today for the hearing. He asks these families to please stand. Judge Miller is nodding his head. Bill introduces these people, and in a louder voice, identifies them by their names…and as *victims* of the scam these defendants perpetrated! They lost their retirement, their savings, and their homes… while these defendants stole their money and lived the high life here and in Hawaii!

Bill is on a roll! Get 'em, Bill! We look over at Beaumont and the Jamesons…they are showing no signs of remorse…whatsoever! Their attorneys have been shifting around a bit, however!

He continued for a few more minutes, detailing the value of the properties, etc., these defendants stole from trusting citizens…over $5,000,000.

Before he finished, Bill, calmly and politely, mentioned the DA in Waikiki had opened an investigation and will be bringing charges against them as well. It is estimated they stole an additional $3,000,000 from the citizens of Hawaii!

Now finished, he returned to his chair. The judge asked the defendants' attorneys if they wanted to add anything. They all said, "No, Your Honor. However, a plea agreement was reached yesterday and should be in their files."

Judge Miller opened each case file and pulled out the *plea agreements*. Oh, boy…here we go!

He looked at the families in the courtroom…then looked at the defendants. He offered his sincere apology to the families and said hopefully he can bring them some resolution.

Now, turning his complete attention to the defendants, he began speaking.

Just last week he had the pleasure of sentencing three of their associates…partners in crime…to a term of twenty years in state prison, plus restitution. He ordered the DA's office to proceed with seizing all the assets of these defendants…Beaumont and the Jamesons…in an effort to return some of the monies to these families…to these victims!

He found what they *all* did…their multiple scams against hardworking people…to be totally despicable! "When it got *too hot* for you here…the law was closing in on you…you simply moved your base of operations to another state…continuing to steal from honest citizens!"

Holding up the *plea agreement* paperwork previously made, Judge Miller, in a somewhat theatrical motion, ripped them in half! Their attorneys tried to look shocked…but they weren't! They had done their best for their clients but knew it was a lost cause!

Judge Miller continued stating his total disgust for these defendants. They showed no shame, no emotion or remorse…nothing! He said his job is to protect the people of this county, this state, from people like them! They belong in a place where they no longer can cause harm to other innocent people.

Therefore, you are sentenced to a term of thirty years in state prison…with no chance of parole…plus restitution. We *will* find where you put all your money! And again, the DA's office has initiated seizing their assets and bank accounts…and will be looking even deeper to find additional *hidden accounts*! We *will find* your money! You will have plenty of time to think about the pain you inflicted on others.

Judge Miller banged his gavel. Declared the bond posted on defendant Beaumont, and previously forfeited by the court, is now exonerated…the liability is clear. The court is now in recess! Very proud!

The bailiff marched them out of the *cage* and back to their holding cells. They weren't looking too *cocky* now! Judith Jameson actually broke out crying…finally realizing how she will be spending the rest of her life.

Bill comes over and shakes hands with Uncle Mike. Says he'll see us later…he has to get back to his office now.

We are all so happy with the outcome. Diane emphasizes that Bill and Judge Miller did a fabulous job! The team, including Marla and myself, are really pleased with the result…considering what we went through to help bring them to justice.

Nelly sees us approaching the office and runs outside to meet us…she can't wait to hear what happened! Uncle Mike gives her a *play-by-play* account of both Bill and Judge Miller…and the thirty-year sentences!

Everyone hangs out for a few more minutes…jibber-jabbering about the morning events…then slowly leaves the office. They need to get home and get some rest…we have a *party tonight*! Nelly reminds everyone it's seven tonight…at Dante's!

Now this is the first time I heard "Dante" mentioned! Good choice, good food, good wine, and wonderful friends and family.

Once everyone is gone, I ask Nelly to help me with something. We need to make a sign for the front door: "We will be closed at 5:00 p.m. today and will reopen tomorrow morning at six thirty."

I have rarely closed the office. However, this is a special occasion…Uncle Mike and my great team. I want everyone there and to have a good time!

CHAPTER 13

The Envelope!

It's two o'clock now…we'll be closing the office in three hours. Nelly says we have two clients scheduled to come in shortly. The bail totals $35,000. She, naturally, has everything ready.

I tell her I'm thinking of heading home a little early…wanting to jump in the shower and get cute for tonight!

We've been so busy, I almost forgot: *the envelope*…the envelope in my safe that has been driving me crazy this last week. I text Uncle Mike and ask him what he wants me to do with it. He simply replies to bring it with me tonight…but *do not open*! Okay…okay!

Nelly kicks me out and says she can handle the new clients… and will drop the bonds off at the jail on her way home. Great!

I get home, turn on some *easy-listening* music, grab a bottle of water from the fridge, and relax on the couch for a few minutes… trying to clear my brain of *everything*. But I can't…I'm too excited about Uncle Mike's party tonight…and the envelope!

All showered, dressed in *nonwork* clothes, and trying to look cute, my cell phone rings. It's David. He wants to know if he and Donny could pick me up for the dinner. Wonderful idea…because I plan on having a few glasses of wine…after all, it's a party! He said they'd see me at six thirty. Good, I have an hour to perfect my makeup! I don't wear makeup to work…I think I've forgotten how to put it on! Still needs some work…not cute enough, yet!

After dabbling around with this makeup stuff for another ten minutes, I step back and look in the mirror. Not bad…acceptable. I do notice, however, that those *laugh lines* will not go away…no matter how I try to conceal them! Oh well, I look somewhat cute!

My chauffeurs arrive right on time. They both come to my door and escort me to their car…walking arm in arm. I even got to sit in the front seat. What gentlemen!

Oh my gosh! I forgot the *envelope*! David helps me out of the car and walks back to the house with me, waiting outside for me, while I run and get the *envelope*. I slip it into my shoulder bag, get back in the car, and head out…on our way to celebrate…everything!

We arrive at Dante's Italian Restaurant right on schedule. Dante comes up and greets us warmly…leading us to the large banquet room. Streamers and balloons are everywhere…how fun. Nelly and Marla have been busy.

Everyone starts showing up. Gina, Darren, Steve, Uncle Mike and Diane, Susie, Marla, Nelly, Bill, Judge Miller, and Dee Dee! My gosh, we have a full house.

Dante brings out ten bottles of wine and sets them on the tables. "This is just to start," he says! I look around the room. Everyone is happy…telling stories, especially about the Waikiki adventure. Uncle Mike is beaming with pride.

Dante goes from table to table, pouring wine for everyone… no empty glasses are allowed. I stand up and raise my glass to toast Uncle Mike. Saying a few words about what a terrific guy he is, how he taught me everything…even how to kick the daylights out of a sandbag! We are so happy to spend this time with him…and Diane. Everyone raises their glass to toast! Just an excuse to drink more wine…works for me!

Donny stands up and walks behind me, placing his hands on my shoulders. He starts saying how we recently celebrated our twenty years in the business…and what a twenty years it has been! He and his team have had the honor, the pleasure, of working with us for only eight years…but *it feels like twenty*! He acknowledges his great team and how vital they *all* are to the success of this business. He's very proud, and knows his team is as well, to be a part of this *family*!

Uncle Mike is still beaming, I'm starting to get a little emotional…this is supposed to be about Uncle Mike, not me!

Dante fills up the glasses, again…keep it coming, Dante! Nelly takes over the floor, stands, and makes *another* toast. "To DJ and Uncle Mike. If it wasn't for Uncle Mike, we wouldn't have DJ!" She goes on to say how she and Marla have been with me the entire twenty years. They were both in need of a job, and I took a chance on them…they will be forever grateful! And she continued, "Look what we have *all* built together. We couldn't think of anywhere else we wanted to be…or anyone else we would ever want to work with!"

I stand up. "Okay…okay…this is a party for Uncle Mike…not me!" Everyone starts yelling at me to sit down and take a sip of wine!

Much to my surprise, Judge Miller…Tony…stands up, with glass in hand…and makes *another* toast. He expresses his deep gratitude to me and my terrific team of investigators! He knows we will always *get our man*…along with other criminals that get in our way. Raising his glass even higher, he mentions the assistance we have provided the county in returning some dangerous individuals to his jurisdiction…giving him the opportunity to mete out their appropriate sentences! Everyone laughs. "Cheers to you all!"

I look over at Uncle Mike, he's still beaming and even getting a little *teary-eyed*! Diane puts her arm around him…also with pride.

With his composure regained, he now stands and thanks everyone…what a pleasure to have such great friends! He makes his way over to me, placing his hands on the back of my chair. He says to me, while winking at everyone else, "The *envelope*, please!"

We're all having so much fun…I completely forgot about the *envelope*! I picked up my shoulder bag and retrieved the *mysterious package* and handed it to him. It's still in the mailing envelope…he shows it to everyone…saying he wanted to make sure I didn't get nosey and try to open it! They all know me too well!

He's standing in the center of the room, surrounded by our friends sitting at their tables. He holds up the *envelope*, pretending to make a big production of *finally* opening it. He asks me to join him. Everyone has big smiles. Dee Dee pushes back her chair a little.

He pulls out *two more* envelopes. I see him nod to Dee Dee. She joins us in the center of the room. She starts expressing her love for all of us...how she's so fortunate to be a part of our *family* these many years. However, as we all know, she is retiring soon...hoping to see the world.

Uncle Mike takes the larger envelope and opens it, straightening out the papers. Dee Dee continues saying that Uncle Mike, after much negotiation, *bought her building and her business*! My knees buckled...and Uncle Mike catches me. He hands me the paperwork: the deed, signed, sealed, and delivered...in my name! I am now the proud owner of the building and the donut shop! However, Dee Dee keeps talking. I can do whatever I want with the building...expand the bail office...keep the donut shop...anything!

I am so shocked, stunned...totally blown away! Everyone starts whooping and hollering! But before we can get too excited, Uncle Mike waves the *second* envelope in the air. Now what...I don't know if I can take much more! Dee Dee gives me a great big hug and returns to her seat.

Diane is now making her way to the center of the room... standing next to Uncle Mike. Switching the envelope from hand to hand, he starts saying how some little *birdies*, he won't mention their names, Nelly and Marla, told him I haven't taken a vacation in over seven years...always working...always taking care of them!

He hands Diane the envelope to open. They both have *great big smiles* on their faces! She hands me the contents! I can't believe what I'm seeing!

A fourteen-day cruise to Italy...for four people! Four people? Uncle Mike jumps in...so excited...and says the ship leaves in seven days and he, Diane, Bill, and I will be on board! We'll see Rome, Pisa, Sicily...and cruise around all the islands! A well-deserved vacation for us all! So...I better start getting packed!

Marla and Nelly rush up to hug me...telling me they can handle the office, which they truly can! Nelly lets it slip that Uncle Mike and Diane have been planning this for the last six months...and she made sure my passport is still valid. I am overcome with joy...and shock. This is all too much to take in!

So, this is what all the whispering has been about? I knew something was up…but never expected all of this!

Bill pulls his chair close to me…saying Mike called him months ago and asked if he would be interested in going on the cruise…with some really fun people. Mike knew he hadn't taken a vacation in quite some time…thanks to Susie! He started laughing, saying it was all they could do to not let the *cat out of the bag*! We'll have so much fun…and we both, definitely, need the break! I wholeheartedly agreed!

Now that our exciting *hoopla* is winding down, Dante brought in a variety of his famous dishes…and more wine! I went over to Uncle Mike…thanked him for *everything*…from the bottom of my heart. Naturally I told him he shouldn't have done it! But he wasn't paying attention to me…he just picked me up and swung me around!

Sitting next to Bill, I whispered I had one last *business* question for him: "What about Caroline Campbell's house? Supposedly her daughter bought it for her. Would the house be included in the *asset*-seizure properties?" He knew me so well…knew I would be asking him about this.

Evidently, he explained, the house was in Caroline's name…they could not prove that Christine bought it for her…no money trail! It appears Caroline told everyone her daughter bought her the house…wanting her neighbors to think her daughter was some sort of *bigwig*! So, she gets to keep her house.

I couldn't be happier! My $150,000 forfeited liability has been cleared; we had an exciting adventure; Uncle Mike has a new *sweetie*; we're going on a cruise to Italy; we have a new office addition; and we got we got *justice for Blake*!

Time to party! One last toast!

To *all* my family and friends!

And…*to our next adventure…wherever it may take us*!

ABOUT THE AUTHOR

Ms. Bollen is a twenty-five-year veteran of the bail industry. She has had the honor of working with the best—and most professional—fugitive recovery agents…a.k.a. bounty hunters. It was such a pleasure to participate in many of the crazy fugitive apprehensions.

The adventures of DJ and her team are the result of these fugitive case apprehensions. The cases provide the *bones* for the adventures.

Ms. Bollen lives on a houseboat in California and enjoys traveling the world with her family and friends.

She looks forward to bringing more excitement and fun to her readers. Lots of stories to still be told! Enjoy!